THE ULTIMATE
DRINKING GAMES
BOOK

THIS IS A CARLTON BOOK

This edition published 1998 for
Parragon Book Service Ltd
Unit 13–17 Avonbridge Trading Estate,
Atlantic Road, Avonmouth
Bristol BS11 9QD

ISBN 0 75252 738 X

Printed and bound by Firmin-Didot (France)
Group Herissey
N° d'impression : 43709

THE ULTIMATE
DRINKING
GAMES
BOOK

Written and compiled by
Dean Evans

SIENA

CONTENTS

INTRODUCTION

OR HOW TO GET DRUNK CLEVERLY
Being a selection of welcoming words and a smattering of rules and regulations to ensure fun for all

There's nothing that livens up an evening out (or indeed 'in') with friends quicker than a good old-fashioned drinking game. Using the random nature of spinning coins, picked cards, tumbled dice, or the character-based quirks of TV characters, you can quickly turn an innocent night's beer-swilling into a fiercely competitive booze-a-thon where the first stop on your hazy ride is Oblivion Central and nobody is allowed to get off. Together with tongue-twisting word games and more traditional pub-based entertainment, over 200 drinking games have been gathered together in this handy reference guide.

There are games that range from the simple (**Beer Mat Catching**); to the daunting (**Kings**) and the terrifying (**Drink Don't Think**). Games that require skill and strategy (**Coin Rugby**); games that demand mental agility (**Fizz Buzz**); and games that necessitate an over-generous chunk of blind luck (see any dice or card game). Everything you could possibly want to know about drinking and drinking games is revealed here in this book. You'll be amazed at the number of games you can play with the change in your pocket, or with a pack of cards. And once you've started, you'll find it difficult to stop. The addictiveness of these games is sky-high and when you've found the game that's right for you, it's difficult to have a 'normal' drink again. Open **The Ultimate Drinking Games Book** and read on...

Important Note: while the drinking games presented in this book are designed to enhance the enjoyment of a night's social drinking, the publishers and the creators of **The Ultimate Drinking Games Book** would like to point out that, while they do encourage hearty boozing, they do NOT, in any way, condone drinking and driving. Or for that matter, drinking and cycling, drinking and vandalism, drinking and operating heavy construction machinery, etc. The games in this book are meant to be fun, and a certain degree of planning must take place before embarking on any one of them. **(1)** Do NOT drive under any circumstances. The very nature of the drinking games here means that you and sobriety will not be friends come the end of the night. **(2)** Take enough money to be able to buy your share of the drink, and to get yourself a cab home when the hilarity winds up. **(3)** Carry a pack of cards, a matchbox, some assorted coinage and a set of five six-sided dice - just in case. **(4)** Stronger drinkers may want to carry a chess set or a small table with them in addition.

* **It is illegal to consume beer and alcohol if you are under the age of 18. So DON'T do it.**

Some basic rules

To enable you and your friends to enjoy an argument-free night of heavy drinking, there are a few simple rules that you should bear in mind:

RULE (1) Each game in **The Ultimate Drinking Games Book** has been carefully categorised and broken down into five separate chunks: **the Title;** the **Essential Supplies** that you'll need to play it; the **Danger Factor** which tells you how easy the game is to play; the **'Bolloxed Factor'** which gives you an indication of how drunk you should be before you start to play it; and the **main description.** A sample layout will look as follows:

* "The Pub Crawl"

* Essential supplies

A large amount of pubs, in a very small area. Money.

* Danger factor/Ease-of-play

A game as old as recorded time. Which is pretty damned old.

* Bolloxed factor

See the following description...

* Hints and tips

Helpful advice, unsurprisingly.

Description

You can gauge how drunk you need to be to play each game by consulting the unique 'Bolloxed Factor', a score out of ten that indicates the perfect degree of confident drunkenness required for playing the game to best effect. The Bolloxed Factor works like so:

The Bolloxed Factor

 1 out of 10

Booze-free. Somebody asks you to spell 'Nefarious'. You get it right and can suggest some synonyms.

 2 out of 10

You've had your first drink. Spelling still isn't a problem.

 3 out of 10

Another drink down the hatch. Spelling isn't on your list of priorities right now, but you can spell 'Nefarious' if you have to.

 4 out of 10

The world's looking hazy. Somebody asks you to spell 'Nefarious'. You say 'N-I-F-A-I-R-E-U-S' and are quite pleased with yourself.

7

5 out of 10

The ugly chick at the end of the bar looks remarkably like Denise Van Outen. You could give spelling 'Nefarious' a good shot, but you need the toilet first.

6 out of 10

Pissed. Somebody asks you to spell 'Nefarious'. You say 'N-I- ah f***it.'

7 out of 10

Wrecked. Somebody asks you to spell 'Nefarious'. You say 'P-I-G'. This is the funniest thing you have ever said.

8 out of 10

Trolleyed. The somebody becomes two somebodies. Both of them ask you to spell 'Nefarious'. You still say 'P-I-G'. When you've stopped laughing they help you up.

9 out of 10

Smashed. The two somebodies ask you to spell 'Nefarious' again. But the enormous pink elephants tell you not to answer the bad people.

 **10 out of 10**

Sozzled. Doctors will later find traces of blood in your alcohol stream. A disembodied voice asks you to spell 'Nefarious'. You can't see or hear anything.

RULE (2) Beer, lager or cider must be drunk from a pint glass or from the original bottles that the drink came in.

RULE (3) Cocktails or spirits must be drunk from a half-pint glass.

RULE (4) The definition of a pint is eight fingers. One or two finger drink penalties can be measured by placing your first two fingers side-by-side on the glass, the first finger at the level of the alcohol remaining. The player must drink enough beer so that the level of the drink drops to below the second finger.

RULE (5) The 'gulp', 'sip' or 'swig' is a bit of a grey area, ranging from a small sip to a big mouthful. Decide which you'll use before you play.

RULE (6) The majority of the games here (unless otherwise specified) are designed to be played with pints of beer. Fines can be halved for those players drinking spirits.

RULE (7) If any player is required to 'down a pint', the drink must be drained completely within 60 seconds.

Additional rules:

* **Players are NOT allowed to point.**

* **Players must drink with their left hand (if right-handed) and vice versa.**

* **The Thumb Master**

One player is elected to be the Thumb Master. At any time during a drinking game, if the Thumb Master places his/her thumb on the table, the other players must do the same when they spot it. The last player to do so, loses the Thumb Master challenge and incurs a drinking forfeit – usually a finger/sip of beer. The losing player then becomes the new Thumb Master.

* **The Jive Master**

One player is elected to be the Jive Master. At any time during a drinking game, if the Jive Master jumps up and 'jives' (i.e. wiggles his/her body around and waves his/her arms erratically) then every player around the table must do the same. Again, the last player to do so loses the Jive Master challenge and incurs a drinking forfeit. The losing player then becomes the new Jive Master.

• The Toilet Master

Sounds disgusting, but it's perfectly innocent. Any player wanting to go to the toilet during the course of a game must ask permission from the Toilet Master. The Bog Lord must then put it to a vote amongst the other players in the group. If the vote is a 'no', the player cannot ask again for ten minutes.

CHAPTER 1

CARD GAMES

Card games have been around for hundreds of years, if not thousands. They have been played for fun, for matchsticks, and most notably for money. By far the best way of using a deck of 52 playing cards is for the wide variety of easy-to-grasp drinking games that we've gathered together on the following pages. With mutated versions of old favourites like **Poker**; the tense, Russian Roulette hell of **Kings**; and the relentless drink-by-the-second torture of **Suits**, making sure you have a pack of cards when you stock up on your beer and spirits will easily spice up a night's raucous alco-quaffing. For some of the games two packs of cards are preferable, but most work with a single deck. Note: the two jokers (four if you use two packs) should always be removed unless specified in the rules – although ultimately it won't matter if you leave them in and treat them as wildcards. Enjoy your drinking and don't do anything we haven't already done.

PRESIDENTS & ARSEHOLES

 INITIALLY TRICKY BUT EASY TO MASTER AFTER THE FIRST FEW ROUNDS.

ESSENTIAL SUPPLIES
A pack of cards. Four players. Enormous quantities of beer or spirits.

Deal out all of the cards in the pack to the players involved - this first hand will eventually determine which of the participants will get the coveted title of **'arsehole'.** The object of the game is to get rid of all of your cards. Play starts with the person on the left of the dealer, aces are high, jokers are wild. **The rules:** players can throw away any one card, or a combination of two, three or even four cards as long as those multiple cards have the same face value (i.e. you can lay down two 3s; three 8s; or if you haven't got any multiple cards, you can discard any single card). The next player must then lay down the same amount of cards as the previous player, but the cards must be of a greater value. **For example,** if player 1 puts down two 9s, player 2 must lay two 10s, jacks, queens, kings, or aces. If the next player lays down the same card as the previous player then the next player misses a go and must drink (one finger). If the following player can't lay down greater cards, then he/she must drink (one finger). The game ends when all cards have been played, or if nobody can lay any more cards. **Now for the twist:** for each hand after the first, a ranking system comes into play – the first person out in the opening hand becomes the **President**, the second becomes the **Vice-President**, the third becomes an executive, the fourth is the proverbial **arsehole**. For the following rounds, anyone who ranks higher then you can tell you

Hints & Tips

Avoid playing this game with maiden aunts and visiting clerics. This game is going to get dirty-mouthed in a hurry.

to drink whenever they want to but there are some special rules: **The Arsehole must always deal the cards**; when all cards have been dealt, **the arsehole must also surrender their two best cards to the President**. Conversely, **the President gives the two worst cards in their hand to the Arsehole**. Play continues until cards become fuzzy and indistinct

Variants: Labour and Conservative; Upper Class and Working Class; but whatever you call this game, the rules remain the same.

Bolloxed factor...

BEERAMID

 ⚠️ OLD GAME, NEW TWIST.

ESSENTIAL SUPPLIES
A pack of cards. Prior knowledge of rudimentary pyramid design. Beer.

Beeramid is an alcoholic variant of the old Pyramid game – the same easy-to-grasp rules, but a greater degree of danger. The dealer lays out 15 cards in a pyramid form (five along the bottom, then four in the next row, etc.) and then gives five cards, face down, to each player. Each card in the **Beeramid** represents one drink (or if you're playing slowly, one finger). Play starts when the dealer flips over the top card in the **Beeramid**. Players then look at their cluster of cards and if the revealed **Beeramid** card is the same number as a card in their hand they can make someone else take a drink. For example, if the flipped card is the 4 of hearts, anyone with the 4 of clubs, spades or diamonds can nominate somebody else to drink. You can also **bluff** that you have the card, when you haven't and the other players must then decide whether to believe you and drink or call your bluff. If you call a player's bluff and he DOESN'T have the card, the bluffer must drink **double**. If you call a player's bluff and he DOES have the card, then you must drink **triple**. Repeat until blasted.

Variants: 30 cards. A bigger pyramid. Know what we're saying?

 Hints & Tips
Bluffers run the greater risk, but the rewards are higher too. We know what we prefer doing…

Bolloxed factor…
🍾🍾🍾🍾🍾🍾🍾

CIRCLE OF DEATH

⚠ **A DANGEROUS GAME WITH THE PROSPECT OF FAST, UNCOMFORTABLY LONG DRINKING.**

ESSENTIAL SUPPLIES
A pack of cards. A large table. Beer.

imple, deadly and effective (but only to be played with cans or pints of beer). Remove the jokers from a pack of playing cards and spread the deck out into a large circle. The dealer then chooses a card from the assembled **Circle Of Death** and reveals it to the other players. The player to the dealer's left picks a second card and also reveals it to the others. If the two cards are of the same suit (i.e a 2 of hearts and a 7 of hearts), add up the values of the two cards (i.e. 2 of hearts and a 7 of hearts = 9) and the two players who picked the cards must drink for the appropriate number of seconds. If the two cards aren't of the same suit, then the first player places their card onto a discard pile and the third person to the dealer's left draws a card. If it matches the suit of the second player's card, then the values of the two cards are combined and the unfortunate players drink for the required number of seconds. Again, repeat until people fall over.

Hints & Tips
Try and ensure that people are drinking at a fairly even rate. You can drink a pint or a finger in 20 seconds...

Bolloxed factor...
🍾🍾🍾🍾🍾🍾🍾

CIRCLES OF MORE DEATH

 A DEADLIER VARIANT OF CIRCLE OF DEATH. MORE CIRCLES = MORE DRINKING.

ESSENTIAL SUPPLIES
A pack of cards. An even larger table. Yet more beer.

ike **Circle of Death, Circles Of More Death** uses the similar match-the-cards gameplay, but ups the danger and the excitement by having more circles and thus even more chances to drink. Arrange the playing cards in three circles, inside one another. The players sit in a circle on the outside of this deadly card-hoop and the player to the dealer's left draws a card. If the player draws a black card, then he/she must drink for X seconds – where X is the value of the drawn card: 1,2, 3, 4, 5, 6, 8, 9, 10; Jack = 10, Queen = 10, King = 10, Ace = 11. If the card drawn is red, however, the player can either allocate the whole number to another player, or split it up and condemn two or more players to drink. When the cards in the outer circle have been exhausted, play moves into the first inner circle where the penalties are doubles (i.e 1=2; 5=10; etc.) Naturally, when play reaches the third and last circle, the penalties are tripled.

 Hints & Tips
Try not to get involved in a vendetta early on. It could cost you dearly in the centre circle.

Bolloxed factor...

DRUG DEALER

A SICK, TWISTED, DECIDEDLY DEADLY GAME THAT MIGHT MAKE YOUR FRIENDS HATE YOU.

ESSENTIAL SUPPLIES
A pack of cards. Beer. More than six players.

Separate X cards (where X is the number of players in the game) from the deck and, ensuring that there is one Ace and one King mixed in with them, deal one card to each person. The players then look at their card, hiding it from the others in the game. The player holding the Ace becomes the **Drug Dealer**, while the player holding the King is the **Cop**. The **Drug Dealer** then has to wink (slyly) at the other players. Any player who sees the wink must then say: "The deal is going down." It is up to the player holding the King, the **Cop**, to try and work out who the **Drug Dealer** is. For each wrong guess, the **Cop** must drink for 5 seconds. Players can bluff and pretend they saw the wink even if they haven't. But if the cop sees the wink, the **Drug Dealer** must drink for 5 seconds and the cards must be re-dealt. This game works best with large groups of people, sat in a large circle or around a table, where the participants can't always see the expressions of the others.

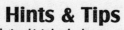

Hints & Tips
Try to avoid playing this in hotels where groups of policemen are staying. Potential embarrassment awaits…

Bolloxed factor…

EIGHTS

 A SIMPLE SET OF RULES HIDES A GAME THAT OPENS A LARGE, CREAKING GATEWAY TO DRUNKENNESS.

ESSENTIAL SUPPLIES
A pack of cards. Beer. Beer. And more beer.

emove the four 8s from a deck of cards, arrange them on a table in a vertical line and then deal the remainder of the cards out to the players. The aim of the game is simply to build up the card suits from 2 to Ace, with alcohol a-penalty for players who can't lay the required cards. For example, player one can put down the 7 of diamonds (or the 9 of diamonds) next to the 8 on the table. He can then force a player of his choice to drink two drinks (or fingers) because there are two cards of the same suit on the table. If player one can't lay down a sequential card, then he can play a card that is as close as possible to the cards on the table – i.e. player one could lay a 5 of clubs next to the 8. But he/she must drink the gap inbetween, in player 1's case the 6 and 7 of clubs; two cards which equals two drinks (or fingers). As the game continues the penalties become greater (when there are thirteen cards in a suit, that's 13 drinks (or fingers) to an unlucky player. Repeat until cards are exhausted. Or you are.

 Hints & Tips
Probably best played with fingers rather than whole drinks for all but the most hardened drinkers.

Bolloxed factor...

20

GIVE OR TAKE

 REQUIRES SOME THOUGHT, SOME MATHS AND THE WATER RETENTION OF A CAMEL.

ESSENTIAL SUPPLIES
A pack of cards. A table. Beer.

Deal out 36 cards, face down, in a 6 by 6 grid, dividing the remaining 16 cards between the players. The only thing to remember is that the first line of the 6 by 6 grid is a '**Give**' row and the drink penalties are from 1-6 fingers counting the cards from left to right. The second line is a '**Take**' row and again, the penalties are from 1-6 fingers. Subsequently, the third row is a '**Give**' and the fourth is a '**Take**' (on both of these rows the penalties are **doubled**, i.e. 2, 4, 6, 8, 10, 12). Likewise, the fifth row is '**Give**' and the sixth is '**Take**' (on both of these rows the penalties are **tripled**, i.e. 3, 6, 9, 12, 15, 18). To play, the first player flips over the top-left card in the grid and whoever has a card of the same value can '**Give**' a one finger penalty to another player. The second card in the grid then gets turned over by the next player, and whoever has a card of a similar value can dish out a two-finger penalty. When play reaches a '**Take**' row, players with a card of the same value as the grid-card revealed must drink the penalty themselves. If nobody has a card that matches the card in the grid, the game moves onto the next one and a higher penalty.

Hints & Tips
Remember to keep all player's cards visible to avoid unseemly arguments and possible violence.

Bolloxed factor...

21

GOLF

 EASY. AND IT HAS ABSOLUTELY NOTHING TO DO WITH SWINGING A CLUB AT A SMALL WHITE BALL.

ESSENTIAL SUPPLIES
A pack of cards. Beer.

Deal four cards to each player, face down. Place the remainder of the pack in the centre of the table and flip over the top card. Players can then choose to look at one of their four cards, but can only look at it once.

Knowing the value of one of the four cards, the aim of the game is to assemble the lowest possible hand. Each player, in turn, can pick up a card from the top of the pack and exchange it for one of their four cards, hoping that the card they throw away is of greater value than the card they replace it with.

This process continues around the table until someone believes that they have the lowest hand in the game. The confident player shouts 'golf' and, **after the rest of the players get one more chance to improve their own hands**, the cards are revealed.

Players then add up the value of their four cards and whoever has the lowest combined total wins the round, by completing the course in the least number, just like golf, y'see? The other players must then drink for a number of seconds equal to the combined value of their cards, calculated using the table on the right. If the person who calls 'golf' does NOT have the lowest hand, the value of their hand is doubled and the game still ends. Whoever DOES have the lowest hand is the winner

Hints & Tips
If you're any good at real golf, don't imagine it's going to help you here. It most certainly won't.

and is spared the need to imbibe. If two or more players tie with the same totals, players must draw single cards out of the deck – the lowest card wins.

Card Values:
Ace=1
King=10
Queen=10
Jack=10
All other cards are scored at face value.

Bolloxed factor...

HI-LO

 THE DRINKER'S EQUIVALENT OF RUSSIAN ROULETTE. IT'S ALL ABOUT LUCK...

ESSENTIAL SUPPLIES
A pack of cards. Beer. Two players only.

While any number of people can play a game of **Hi-Lo**, only two can take part at any one time. After choosing a **Dealer** and a **Player**, shuffle a pack of cards and let the dealer turn over the top card. The **Player** must then decide whether the next card will be higher or lower than the card revealed by the **Dealer**. For every card guessed correctly, the dealer drinks one finger/sip. For every card guessed wrong, the **Player** must drink. The game continues until the next card turned over matches the value of the original card turned over by the dealer. If the **Player** guesses the following card correctly, he/she is allowed to leave the game and can nominate a replacement. If the **Player** guesses incorrectly, the **Dealer** is allowed to leave. Repeat as many times as humanly possible.

Variants:
See **Red And Black**.

 **Hints & Tips**
Avoid playing this game with Bruce Forsyth, or anybody who claims to do a good impression of him.

Bolloxed factor...

24

PYRAMID

⚠ **A GAME INVOLVING ABSOLUTELY NO SKILL WHATSOEVER.
DO YOU FEEL LUCKY? WELL DO YA?**
ESSENTIAL SUPPLIES
A pack of cards. Beer. Knowledge of the basic 'pyramid' shape.

Like the **Beeramid**, shuffle a pack of cards and deal out 15 cards in a rough pyramid shape – five at the base, four on top of that, then three, two and one. The aim of the game is to start with the bottom-left card and to work your way up the pyramid (left to right) without turning over a **Jack, Queen, King** or **Ace**. Cards with a value from 2-9 incur no penalty. If a player turns over a 10, the penalty is one finger/sip, but he/she can carry on. If a player turns over a picture card or an **Ace**, they pay a bigger penalty (Jack = 2 fingers, Queen = 3, King = 4, Ace = 5) and the game stops. At which point everyone else must have a drink. All of the flipped cards are then replaced with fresh, unseen cards and the player must begin again, from the bottom. Repeat until the pyramid is beaten, or until the players are lying in a drunken heap on the floor trying to sing Japanese Opera. You'll know when it's time to give up...

Hints & Tips
The trick in this game is to know when to push your luck and when not to. Don't go too far, let someone else.

Bolloxed factor...
🍾🍾🍾🍾🍾🍾🍾🍾🍾

KINGS

⚠ **PERFECTLY PLAYABLE AND ENJOYABLE. UNLESS YOU DRAW THE LAST OF THE FOUR KINGS...**

ESSENTIAL SUPPLIES
A pack of cards. A jug, or large cup. Beer.

 ut an empty jug, a vase (without flowers in it), a bucket or a large cup in the middle of the table. Deal a deck of cards in a circle around it. Then, starting with the player on the dealer's left, each person draws a card from the circle. Each card has its own particular consequences:

Ace:
Everyone drinks one finger/sip from their drinks.

2-5:
The player drawing the card drinks from 2-5 fingers/sips depending on the value of the card.

6-9:
The player drawing the card nominates another player to drink from 6-9 fingers/sips depending on the value of the card.

10:
The players to the left and right of the person who draws the 10, must drink ten fingers/sips.

Jack:
The person who picks a Jack must quickly think of a topic, i.e. football,

Hints & Tips

Just DON'T draw the fourth King. When three are down the tension can become unbearable. The Toilet Master has a clear advantage here.

cars, etc., and then each player must think of a type, i.e. Liverpool, Audi. Anyone who hesitates or makes a mistake drinks ten fingers/sips.

Queen:

Grants you temporary safety, do NOT drink for one turn.

King:

When the first King appears, the player must pour the contents of his/her drink into the empty jug/vase/whatever. The same thing happens when the second and third kings appear. When the fourth king is revealed, the unfortunate player adds his/her drink to the jug and must then drink the contents of it. This game takes on a whole new danger if each player is armed with a different drink. Vodka mixed with Gin, Guinness and Beer is not a pretty sight...

Variants:

See **The King's Cup**.

Bolloxed factor...

27

RED AND BLACK

⚠ ANOTHER GAME THAT REQUIRES NO THOUGHT TO PLAY. A 50/50 CHANCE WHETHER YOU DRINK OR NOT.

ESSENTIAL SUPPLIES
A pack of cards. A table. Beer.

Place the cards, face down, in a pile in the centre of a table and decide on the number of cards that each player will draw from it (i.e. 10, 15, 20). Simply guess whether the top card will be black or red and then turn it over. If you are correct nominate another player to drink X fingers/sips (where X is the value of the card drawn). If the guess is incorrect, you must drink the required number of fingers/sips. As usual, picture cards equal ten, and the Ace is high.

Variants:
See **Hi-Lo.**

 **Hints & Tips**
Eat well before you play this game. You may stay quite sober, you may get very drunk indeed.

Bolloxed factor...

SUITS

⚠ **HOW SLOWLY CAN YOU COUNT? THE SLOWER THE BETTER IN THIS GAME.**

ESSENTIAL SUPPLIES
A pack of cards. A table. Beer. Some foolhardy friends.

Another simple game guaranteed to set you up on the fast train to Bladderedville. Gather a group of foolhardy players together and sit in a circle. Nominate a player to be the dealer. **The dealer** calls a suit (diamonds, clubs, spades or hearts) and then deals out the cards, face up, to the players. When a card is dealt that matches the suit nominated by the dealer, the unlucky recipient must drink for the number of seconds shown by the card (picture cards = 10, Ace = 11). The player to the drinker's right must count down the penalty. When the drinker has finished, he/she must choose another suit to continue the game before putting their drink down. If they fail to do this, they receive a further four second drinking penalty. Simple, but effective.

Variants:

Try adding another useful rule – if the player who's counting down the penalty finishes counting before the punished player has finished the beer in their glass, they incur an automatic four-second drinking penalty. As long as somebody else spots it.

Hints & Tips

When you're being forced to drink, keep your mind on the card suit you're going to select next.

Bolloxed factor...

🍾🍾🍾🍾🍾🍾🍾🍾

UP THE RIVER DOWN THE RIVER

⚠ **ANOTHER SKILL-FREE DRINK-A-THON THAT RELIES ON LARGE DOLLOPS OF LUCK.**

ESSENTIAL SUPPLIES
A pack of cards. Beer. A table. A river (just kidding).

A variant of the 'give' and 'take' idea that characterises so many drinking games, **Up And Down The River** is a game that requires very little skill, but a ton of blind, unthinking luck. Begin by nominating a dealer.

The dealer then dishes out four cards, face up, to each player in the game. Picking up a card from the remainder of the pack, the dealer shows it to the other players and invites them to 'take one'. Anybody who has a card with the value shown on the dealer's card, must drink one finger/sip – unless you have two cards of the same value, whereupon the penalty is doubled. If nobody has a card that matches the dealer's card, the dealer drinks. The game then continues with the effective tactic of doubling the penalty...

Picking up another card from the remainder of the pack, the dealer again shows it to the other players and invites them to 'take two'. Anybody who matches the value on the dealer's card, then drinks two fingers/sips. Round three increases the penalty again to 'take three', while the next bumps it up to 'take four'. After this round, the penalty

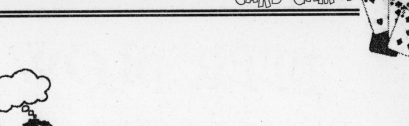

Hints & Tips

Should it become impossible for the dealer to say 'take one', it's probably time to stop. Although hand-held signs are acceptable.

becomes 'give four', decreasing to 'give three', 'give two' and 'give one' with subsequent rounds. Finally, the sequence is reset and begins anew with 'take one'. Repeat for as long as it's funny.

Bolloxed factor...

BEER BLOW

⚠ A GAME OF SKILL, CUNNING AND PURSED LIPS. GENTLY DOES IT.

ESSENTIAL SUPPLIES
A pack of cards. A beer bottle.

If the simple games are always the best, then **Beer Blow** rides high with the greatest drinking games ever invented. Not only is it a chance to embarrass yourself in a multitude of ways (drink yourself into a stupor, blow too soft, blow too hard, and so on) but it also requires a tiny degree of skill and control, something that lessens with each hilarious game. It's ludicrously straightforward: put a pack of cards on top of an empty beer bottle (remember to take the cards out of the pack first – otherwise the game takes longer and it's no fun). Each player then takes it in turn to blow off at least one card from the precariously balanced pack. Funnily enough, the player who blows the last card or cards off of the bottle has to pay the penalty – either two fingers/sips of beer; drinking for five seconds or downing a whole pint. Whatever works best for you.

Hints & Tips
Make sure you clean your teeth before going out to play this one, it can be a motorway to Halitosis City.

Bolloxed factor...

DICTATOR

 A SELFISH POWER GAME, SIMILAR TO PRESIDENTS AND ARSEHOLES.

ESSENTIAL SUPPLIES
A pack of cards. Beer. A mean streak.

A power game that can be as gentle or as deadly as the people who play it. Each player draws a card from the pack. The player with the highest card becomes the **Dictator** and so he/she can define the rules of play for the round (to avoid arguing, it's advisable to write these down). For example, the **Dictator** might want to decree that everybody holding a red card must drink two fingers of beer; that players holding a 7 should sing the national anthem; or that players holding two of a kind, should remove an item of clothing. **Dictators** are encouraged to be as creative as possible in their choice of rules and conditions (if you don't, somebody else undoubtedly will). Play begins as the **Dictator** deals up to five cards to each player. As each card is dealt, the rules are consulted and the appropriate penalties administered. The **Dictator** should also receive a hand of cards, although instead of taking the penalties, the **Dictator** can give them out to the other players. When all five cards have been dealt and the penalties have been executed, the round ends and the Dictatorship passes onto the player to the dealer's left. He/she shuffles the pack, reinvents the rules and deals again...

 Hints & Tips
To stop time-wasting, try and decide what your orders might be before you get into power.

Bolloxed factor...

BRAIN DAMAGE

⚠ **A BIT LIKE BLACKJACK BUT PLAYED TO A MAGICAL 7.5 RATHER THAN 21.**

ESSENTIAL SUPPLIES
A pack of cards. Spirits. Shot glasses.

rab a pack of playing cards and remove all of the 8s, the 9s and the two **red** tens. **Brain Damage** plays much like the Casino game **Blackjack,** in that you start with one card and attempt, by being dealt extra cards, to amass a score as close to 7.5 as possible. Picture cards are worth half-a- point (0.5), Aces a point (1.0), 10s are wild, while cards 2-7 retain their face values.

Cut the pack to see which player goes first (highest card wins) – each person in the game must deal at least once. The dealer then takes the pack and, like traditional **Blackjack,** deals one card face down to the first player and then one to himself. Both players ante up (i.e. bet a drink – spirits in shot glasses tend to work better than beer in this game). The player then looks at the card and gets a chance to ask for extra cards to augment his hand, trying to get as close to the magical 7.5 as possible. If the player goes 'bust' (i.e. goes over 7.5) he/she must drink the bet made.

If the player 'sticks' (i.e. has a hand with a combined total of 7.5 or less), the dealer can then take more cards to try and make his score 7.5 or less. If the dealer busts, he drinks the bet. If both player and dealer stick, extra bets can be made before the two hands are revealed. The

Hints & Tips

Having everybody bring along a different kind of spirit adds variety and at least two to the Bolloxed Factor in this game.

loser (whoever has the lowest score) drinks the bet. In the event of a tie, the dealer wins and the player drinks. As in Blackjack, a five card trick (five cards totalling 7.5 or less) cannot be beaten.

Bolloxed factor...

35

LANDMINE

⚠ **ALSO KNOWN AS ASTEROIDS AND DRUNK DRIVER. THE NAME MAY CHANGE, THE GAME IS STILL THE SAME.**

ESSENTIAL SUPPLIES
A pack of cards. A table. Beer.

Another simple game for two players. Cut the pack to see who becomes the dealer and who becomes the **soldier** (highest card wins). The dealer then places six cards, face down, in front of the soldier. Like the **Pyramid** game, the idea is to move from left to right down the line of cards (the minefield), turning each one over and enduring the drink-related consequences. And they are: If the card is numbered 2-10 then nothing happens. The **soldier** may move onto the next card in the minefield without penalty. If the card is a picture card or an Ace, additional cards are added to the minefield and a mine explodes. The number of cards added is based on the following system: Jack = +1 card, Queen = +2 cards, King = +3 cards, and Ace = +4 cards. And to simulate the mine exploding, the soldier must also drink X fingers of beer (where X is the number of cards the player was penalised with, i.e. +3 = 3 fingers of beer). The **soldier** continues in this manner until (a) he/she is roaring drunk and unable to think or (b) manages to make it to the end of the line of cards. Whereupon another foolhardy **Landmine** challenger can step up.

 Hints & Tips

To make the game even more tricky, just add more cards to the initial minefield, but not too many.

Bolloxed factor...

🍾🍾🍾🍾🍾🍾🍾🍾

MULTI

 A LONG LIST OF RULES. BUT A LONG LIST OF HILARIOUS CONSEQUENCES.

ESSENTIAL SUPPLIES
A pack of cards. Beer. A large group of unwary friends.

Spread all 52 cards in the pack, face down and in no particular pattern, on a table. The first player then simply flips over one of the cards and faces the consequences. In essence, **Multi** is a springboard that leaps the game into a variety of other drinking games. Pick your favourites from this book and simply assign them, as below, to the various card types. Players then continue to pick cards until all 52 have been exhausted, whereupon the pack is reassembled, shuffled and spread out haphazardly once more.

Sample actions:
Ace: Everybody drinks. **King:** Play **Beer Blow.**
Queen: Play **Categories. Jack:** Play **Questions.**
10: Shotgun a beer. **9:** Play **Thumper. 8:** Play **Boat Race.**
7: Play **Beeramid. 6:** Make up any rule.
5-2: Drink X fingers (where X is the value of the card).

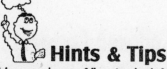 **Hints & Tips**
Make sure you've got a full evening ahead of you before you start a game, this may take some time.

Bolloxed factor....

37

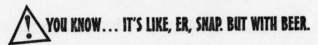

SNAP

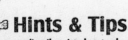 **YOU KNOW... IT'S LIKE, ER, SNAP. BUT WITH BEER.**

ESSENTIAL SUPPLIES
A pack of cards. Beer. Quick hand/eye coordination.

An adult, beer-soaked mutation of the harmless kid's game, **Snap** requires speed of thought, sharp reflexes and the stamina of a large Bison. The nominated dealer shuffles the pack of cards (having two packs mixed together works even better) and places the pile face down on the table. One by one, while the other players sit with one hand behind their backs (the **Snap Hand**), the dealer flips over the cards. When a player spots two cards of the same value in a row, he/she must slam their **Snap Hand** on the discard pile yelling **'Snap'**. The first person to do this is then able to give out the drink penalty (usually the value of the card in seconds of drinking time) to another player in the group. Picture cards are worth 10, Aces 1 or 11 (depending on how brave you are) and play ends when the dealer runs out of cards. The game can be spiced up and the drinking made more frequent by altering the rules so that **'Snap'** can be called when cards are the same suit, or when they are sequential.

Hints & Tips
Don't choose an ordinarily quiet place to play this game, as you'll all be yelling like crazy by the end.

Bolloxed factor...

QUEENS

 SENTENCE YOURSELF TO THE DEPTHS OF DRUNKENNESS WITH THE TURN OF A CARD. NOW… IT'S LIKE, ER, SNAP. BUT WITH BEER.

ESSENTIAL SUPPLIES
A pack of cards. Men. Women. Beer.

Short, sweet but oh-so addictive. **Queens** is a gender game that knows no boundaries. Again, shuffle a pack of cards and place the pack in the centre of the table. Each player, starting to the dealer's left, takes a turn and picks up the top card from the pile. If the card is a **Jack** then all of the male players in the game must drink. If the card is a **Queen,** all of the female players in the game must drink. Additionally, if the card is a **King,** all of the players must drink, and if the card drawn is an **Ace,** members of the opposite sex to the player who drew the card, must drink. There are no penalties for cards **2-10**. Unless, of course, you feel that the game is a touch slow for your liking and you want to make some up. Feel free, that's how new drinking games get invented...

 Hints & Tips
Unscrupulous gentlemen have been known to play the game with two decks and remove a couple of Jacks…

Bolloxed factor...

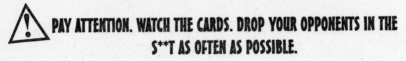

MEXICALI

⚠ PAY ATTENTION. WATCH THE CARDS. DROP YOUR OPPONENTS IN THE
S**T AS OFTEN AS POSSIBLE.

ESSENTIAL SUPPLIES
A pack of cards. Beer (or Tequila for that authentic feel).

Deal out all 52 cards, face down, to the players involved in the game. Starting with the player on the dealer's left, turn over a card. Nothing will happen until player two, perhaps even player three flips over their cards.

The rules are fairly straightforward and best explained by a quick description of a game. So here's an example of the twisted **Mexicali** gameplay: let's say that player one turns over the 4 of spades.

Player two is next up and he reveals the 9 of spades. If he spots that both cards are of the same suit **before** he plays his own card, player three can then start counting to 13 (4 of spades + 9 of spades) while both players one and two drink for the duration of the count.

When they've finished, player three draws his card: the ace of clubs. As this card isn't directly related to the previous two in value or suit, nothing happens. But when player four draws the ace of diamonds, player five can start counting to 28 (Jack = 11, Queen = 12, King = 13, Ace = 14) while player three and four, who both have related aces worth 14 seconds, drink for the duration of the count.

If player five was then to draw the 10 of diamonds, player six could start

Hints & Tips
Playing this game wearing sombreros is recommended to add that extra Mexican feel. And no-one notices when you pass out.

counting to 24 (ace = 14 + 10) while players four and five drink. Repeat until life makes no sense. If you see Snooker on the TV and find it mesmerising, it's probably time to stop.

Bolloxed factor...

41

TRAPPED

 IMAGINE THE TRADITIONAL GAME OF 'IT' BUT WITH CARDS AND BEER.

ESSENTIAL SUPPLIES
A pack of cards. 3-6 players. Beer.

 huffle a pack of cards and divide all 52, face down, between the players. The players are allowed to look at their cards but should keep them **hidden** from the prying eyes of the others in the group.

Beginning with the person sat to the left of the dealer, the player can lay down any card he/she wishes; the 8 of hearts, for example. The next player must then lay down a card of the same face value; in this case, another 8. If the player cannot do so, he/she becomes **'trapped'** and must drink one finger/sip or whatever penalty is deemed necessary.

The drinker then loses that go and the game passes onto the next player, who can now lay any card that they want. If the player that is currently **'trapped'** doesn't have an equal card to match this new card, they remain trapped and drinking.

Play then reverses back to the player on the other side of the trapped player, who lays another new card. If the trapped player still cannot match it with an equal card, he/she drinks again, and the game passes to the player on the other side. This continues until the player is freed and then play continues to move clockwise around the circle until another player finds themselves trapped. When a player has laid his/her last card, the game stops. The other players count up their remaining

Hints & Tips

This is a good starter game for an evening of alcohol indulgence as the drinking's fairly steady, but not too heavy.

cards (NOT the value of their cards) and take the required number of drinks. Finally, the winner collects the cards, shuffles and deals again. The game then begins anew.

Bolloxed factor...

CHEERS!

THE KING'S CUP

⚠ **AN EASY GAME (UNLESS YOU'RE THE POOR SOD THAT HAS TO DRINK THE CONTENTS OF THE CUP AT THE END).**

ESSENTIAL SUPPLIES
A pack of cards. A large cup. Beer.

ike the game **Kings,** place an empty cup in the middle of the table. Deal a deck of cards, face down, in a circle around it. Then, starting with the player on the dealer's left, each person draws a card from the circle. Naturally, each card in the circle has its own particular consequences:

Kings: The King's Cup. Pour some of your drink into **"The King's Cup"** in the middle of the table and then draw another card. Like **Kings,** play continues until the second and third kings appear (more drink is added to the **King's Cup**) and finally the fourth, whereupon the unfortunate player adds some of his/her drink to the Cup and must then drink the contents of it. The game then ends.

Queens: Category cards. Like the stand-alone drinking game **Categories,** the player that draws a Queen card gets to specify a distinct category, i.e types of car, colours, US states, etc. Then, moving in a clockwise direction around the table, players must name an item that fits into the category called by the first player. If a player cannot think of a suitable item or names an item that is not part of the category specified by the original player, then he/she loses the game and must drink. Player discretion (and a good old-fashioned vote) can settle any

Hints & Tips

This is a game that can easily end up with one player absolutely bolloxed. Make sure that isn't you. Unless you like being absolutely bolloxed.

arguments about items and their appropriate categories. No repeats. As always, the majority rules.

Jacks: Rhymes cards. The player that drew the Jack says a word (i.e. sore) and, moving in a clockwise direction, the next player must then say a word that rhymes (i.e. more, score, draw, law, and so on). This process is repeated around the table until a player either can't think of a word that rhymes or says a rhyme that is NOT a recognised word. Repeats are not allowed. Dictionaries can be used to settle any arguments, but a vote should clear up any arguments. Needless to say, the losing player has to drink.

Ace: Rules cards. Picking a Rule card allows the drawing player to make up any rule (the crazier the better) to spice up the proceedings. These can range from the simple (no laughing) to the absurd (players must lay down on their backs while drinking penalties), and from the tricky (no mentioning the word 'and') to the provocative (players must remove all their clothes and stand outside for ten seconds if they draw a three).

10s: Social cards. Easy. Everybody drinks.

(continued overleaf)

45

9s: To the Left. The player to the left of the person that drew the 9 takes a drink.

7s: 7 seconds. The player who drew the 7 can cruelly pick upon any other player, forcing them to drink their drink for 7 seconds.

6s: To the Right. The player to the right of the person that drew the 6 takes a drink.

2s: Drink & draw again. Take a drink and then draw another card and face the consequences.

Bolloxed factor...

GO FISSH

 EXTREMELY DEADLY IF YOU PLAY GO FISH. PUZZLING IF YOU DON'T.

ESSENTIAL SUPPLIES
A pack of cards. Beer. A keen knowledge of the card game Go Fish.

 o Fissh is the alcoholic variant of the children's card game, **Go Fish.** So, if you know the rules to that game and want to add a little boozy spice to an otherwise innocent pastime, try playing it with the following little extras:

(1) If you ask another player for a card and they DON'T have it, drink one finger/sip and **'go fish'.**

(2) If you **'go fish'** and you manage to **'fish your wish'**, then you can make the player drink double the value on the card.

(3) If you ask a player for a card and they DO have it, then that person must drink the value of the card – either in fingers/sips or in seconds.

Hints & Tips

Probably best to avoid playing this with any children. Social Services might get the wrong idea.

Bolloxed factor...

🍾🍾🍾🍾🍾🍾

POKER-HEAD

⚠ **ANOTHER BEER-DRENCHED VERSION OF RUSSIAN ROULETTE. BUT FUNNIER.**

ESSENTIAL SUPPLIES
A pack of cards. Beer. Your head.

ot a game of skill, but literally a game of blind luck, **Poker-head** takes the bidding basis of the famous card game, and whittles it down to a simplicity that even someone with seven pints of lager, three Gin and Tonics and a bottle of wine inside them, can understand. Simply, shuffle the pack and deal one card to each player, face down.

Next, without peeking to see what the card is, each player must pick up their card and place it, with the face visible, on their foreheads. Held there for the duration of the game by a strategically-placed finger, the aim of **Poker-head** is straightforward – whoever has the lowest value card pressed against their noggin is the loser. You know what everybody else has because you can see them. But have no idea what card you have been dealt with. Starting to the left of the dealer, each player bets a number of drinks, or fingers/sips if you're playing with pints, that they have the highest card. This continues from player to player until play ends with a bet from the dealer. Players can fold at any time during the bidding, but must drink the current amount of drink previously wagered.

When all bets are placed, the players are allowed to look at their own cards. Whichever player has the lowest value cards loses the game, and has to drink the accumulated bet.

Hints & Tips

If your teetotal friends from a freaky religious sect come round unexpectedly, you can just play this for money – they're sure to love it!

Variants: Try playing **Poker-head** with more than one card. But instead of holding several cards to your forehead, place one there and keep the other 1-4 in front of you. If using an extra four cards, normal five card poker rules apply and the loser is the player with the worst poker hand.

Bolloxed factor...

CHEERS!

NINES

 UNUSUAL AMONGST DRINKING GAMES BECAUSE IT REQUIRES SOME THOUGHT. ALTHOUGH NOT MUCH.

ESSENTIAL SUPPLIES
A pack of cards. Beer. A good head for numbers.

Nines is a much more demanding game than many card-based drink-a-thons, and one that requires a fair degree of skill and thought. So if that last sentence seemed a bit long to you, and you lost concentration halfway through reading it, you should probably give up now. Or find an adult to help you.

Start by nominating a dealer, who dishes out four cards to each player around the table. The remainder of the pack is left in a pile in the centre of the table, the top card of which is turned over and placed next to it. The aim of the game is to keep track of the cards in this new pile, with each card scoring a certain number of points: i.e. **2-10** score their face value, **picture cards** are also worth **10**, while **Aces** are worth **11**. Each player takes it in turn to place one of the cards from their hand onto the small pile, adding the value of the starting card to the one that they lay on top of it. When the running total of the pile has a 9 in it (9, 19, 29, 39, 49 etc.) the player laying the card can challenge any other player to drink. However, if the challenged player doesn't believe that the total has a 9 in it, he can claim that the player who has challenged him is lying. A quick count will decide who's right and who's wrong (although the counting may actually take quite a while by the end of an evening) – if the challenger is proved right, the player challenged must drink double; likewise if the challenger has got the total wrong, he/she must drink double. The game continues until the pile totals 99 or more.

Hints & Tips

This game can be a teensy bit slow (especially if no-one's any good at maths), so consider playing one of the variants, to give it a twist.

Variants: To up the frequency of drinking opportunities, try **Nine-To-Five,** where players drink if the total ends in a 9 or a 5. Similarly **Odds,** where players drink if the total is an odd number, or **Evens,** where players glug it down if the total is even, liven up the game tremendously.

Bolloxed factor...

CHEAT

 ONE OF THE MOST FUN GAMES YOU CAN PLAY, GIVEN AN EXTRA ALCOHOLIC EDGE...

ESSENTIAL SUPPLIES
A pack of cards. Beer. A suspicious nature.

A fantastic game with or without the drinking aspect (so it works just as well when you've run out of money at the end of the night), **Cheat** is a game of skill, daring and bare-faced lying. The dealer distributes a pack of cards amongst the players, who must lie, cheat and scheme to be the first one to get rid of all their cards. As each player has a wide array of cards, there will doubtless be some of the same value – two 3s, three Queens, and so on. The idea is to lay down these card groups as quickly as possible, whether you have them or not.

For example in a four-player game, player one might announce that he/she is putting down 'two 6s'. Player two could follow this by saying 'one 3'. Player three might chip in with 'two Kings', while player four might mutter 'three 2s'. In a perfect world, each of the four players would have put down exactly the cards that they said they did – i.e. two 6s, one 3, two Kings, and three 2s. But in **Cheat,** you don't have to do what you say. In fact, you're encouraged not to. You just have to make the other players believe that you've laid down the right cards. Going back to the example, player one could have lied and laid a 7 and a 3 (either because he/she had two 6s and didn't want to use them, or had no pairs and wanted to get rid of cards quickly). Player two, by laying a single 3 is obviously not lying (but it's a slow way to get rid of your cards). Player three, like player one could have laid down the cards

Hints & Tips
It's important to only show the top card of the group you're laying down. If you feel extra-sneaky, put down more cards than you say you are.

he/she specified, but could be bluffing. While player four, dumping three of a kind, is either truthful or confidently bluffing.

Shouting **'Cheat'** when a player lays what you believe are suspect cards, is the only way to catch them. If they have lied, the player must drink a penalty and takes his cards back. If they haven't, the accuser must drink the penalty and gains the cards the last player put down. The game continues until someone manages to get rid of all their cards. The losers then count up the number of cards left in their hands, and drink for the appropriate number of seconds.

Bolloxed factor...

TEN BROWN BOTTLES

 MUSICAL CHAIRS (BUT OBVIOUSLY WITHOUT THE MUSIC AND THE CHAIRS).

ESSENTIAL SUPPLIES
A pack of cards. Some empty beer bottles (specifically, one less than the number of players involved in the game).

he alcoholic variant of **Musical Chairs** (but obviously without the music and the chairs), **Ten Brown Bottles** is a game that may end in physical violence. As is nearly always the case with the best of them, the idea is a simple one:

The dealer dishes out four cards, face down, to each player (including himself), placing the rest of the pack in a neat pile, again face down, in the centre of the table. The empty beer bottles, one less than the number of participants, are also placed in the centre of the table. With the scene set, the game can begin. To win, players have to juggle their cards until they have either four of a kind (say, four Kings, four 3s, etc.) or a sequential 'straight' in the same suit (i.e. 3, 4, 5, 6 of hearts; 9, 10, J, Q of clubs). But changing cards is the tricky bit. The dealer picks a card off the top of the pile (without showing it to anybody) and decides whether or not to keep it in his/her hand. Whatever card the dealer chooses to discard, he gives it to the player to his/her left. This player must then choose to discard one of the five cards that they hold, again giving the one that they don't want to the next player. When the play reaches the last person before the dealer, the unwanted card gets placed in a new pile next to the pile of cards already on the table. This

Hints & Tips
Once you start losing this game it becomes increasingly difficult to play (as your reactions slow), so be alert in the early rounds.

process continues until one player has either four of a kind or straight, whereupon he/she makes a grab for a beer bottle in the middle of the table. When this happens, the other players must quickly make a play for the other bottles and the loser is the player that is left without a bottle after this bottle-grabbing free-for-all. As usual, the loser must drink a hefty alcohol-related penalty. Either a pint, or a large shot of something without a mixer.

Bolloxed factor...

CHEERS!

CHAPTER 2

MONEY GAMES

E ven if you can't lay your hands on a pack of playing cards, all you really need to explore some very fine drinking games is a pocket of loose change and very few inhibitions. Reading through the 14 choice diversions gathered here, you'll be amazed how a pile of coins (pennies, 2-pences, 5-pences and 10-pences), can be used to enhance the late-night alcohol experience. In the games below, for example, you'll discover how to play football with 4p and rugby with 2p; how to 'shuffle' a stack of 1p pieces; and which coins have the best aerodynamics and bounceability. In our experience, the answer to this last question is the tiny 5-pence piece, a triumph of lightweight construction that seems to take brilliantly to the group of 'chucking-coins-at-tables' games. So, be popular, liven up a dull night out at your local watering hole with a few bouts of **Anchorman, Chandeliers** or **Taps.** All of them are drinking games beyond compare.

THE ONE COIN GAME

⚠ **SIMPLE YET DEADLY. ESPECIALLY IF YOU PLAY IT FOR MORE THAN TWO HOURS. AND ARE UNLUCKY.**

ESSENTIAL SUPPLIES
A coin. A table. Beer.

Simple but deadly if played for more than an hour, **The One Coin Game** involves gathering a group of friends around a table and nominating an honorary coin-flipper. The game unfolds thus: the designated money-chucker spins the coin into the air, while the player to the left of the flipper has to guess whether it will land on heads or tails. If they manage to get it right, they become the coin-flipper for the player to the left of them. If they get it wrong, they must rush a two-finger/sip fine and are forced to face another 'heads' or 'tails' flip. Only when the player guesses the upturned face of the coin correctly, do the coin-flipping duties move onwards and he/she is saved from further penalty guzzling.

Hints & Tips
Remember to keep a good supply of coins as you'll probably lose quite a few behind benches and down cleavages.

Bolloxed factor...

MULTIPLE COIN SPIN

⚠ **THE TABLETOP EQUIVALENT OF SPINNING PLATES ON STICKS. BUT WITHOUT THE PLATES AND THE STICKS.**

ESSENTIAL SUPPLIES
A stack of coins. A table. Beer.

 simple game, enhanced by the sneaky addition of increasingly higher alcoholic stakes. Make sure you have a big stack of coinage and a clear table, for the aim of this game is simply this: how many coins can you spin simultaneously on a tabletop? Four? Five? Player one, for example, might bet that he/she can spin three coins at the same time. If successful, the stakes can then be raised higher. But if he/she fails in spinning the number of coins bet, the unfortunate change-spinner has to drink X fingers/sips of beer (where X is the number of coins that the player tried to spin). The betting moves clockwise around the table, anybody unwilling to take the challenge must drink the current penalty. This goes on until somebody foolishly tries to spin 14 coins at once and is forced to drink 14 fingers/sips of beer as a punishment. How high can you take it? How many coins can YOU spin?

Hints & Tips
Practice this at home and see how many you can do. "A man's gotta know his limitations," as Clint Eastwood said.

Bolloxed factor...

59

THE TWO COIN GAME

⚠ A GAME OF COIN-FLICKING SUPERSKILLS AND TREMENDOUS DRINKING STAMINA.

ESSENTIAL SUPPLIES
Two identical coins. A matchbox. A table. Beer.

An easy game to play if you're out in the pub (and an obvious sequel to **The One Coin Game**). Simply rifle your pockets for two identical coins – a couple of 10-pence pieces or some 2-pence pieces seem to work the best. Players then gather around a table and take it in turns to flick the two coins from BELOW the level of the table onto the top of the table (pile the two coins together on your thumb and forefinger to get a truly random result). When the coins clatter to a standstill on the table, consult the following drink-related rules and pay the appropriate consequences:

(1) If one coin lands on **'heads'** and the other on **'tails',** the current coin-flicker suffers no penalty and the matchbox (merely a symbol of whose turn it is, rather than an integral part of the whole proceedings) is passed on to the next player in the circle.

(2) If **both** coins land on **'tails',** however, the unfortunate player is forced to down two fingers/sips of beer.

(3) Conversely, if **both** coins land on **'heads',** the coin-flicker is allowed to make up an additional rule to spice the game up (the sillier, the better).

Hints & Tips

Make sure to use any new rule to your advantage. If you're well coordinated, make everyone flip from a metre away, for instance.

(4) If either of the two coins land on the floor, the player who flicked them so inexpertly must suffer a four-finger/sip fine.

Variants:

Ever heard of **The Three Coin Game?** Or **The Four Coin Game?** Obviously, once you can play this simple drinking game with two coins, the rules for these two variants pretty much explain themselves.

Bolloxed factor...

PENNIES

⚠ **REQUIRES GOOD HAND/EYE COORDINATION. PSYCHIC ABILITY AN ADVANTAGE.**

ESSENTIAL SUPPLIES
11 pennies (1-pence pieces). A table. Beer.

Known as **Dimes** in America, the coin game **Pennies** plays much like a traditional card game (it also works equally as well with distinctively designed beer mats, which may be easier to come by). Best played with five players or less, every player gets a chance to **'deal'** the coins. The dealer simply gathers all 11 pennies in his/her hand, shakes them about a bit, and then forms a neat little stack which is then placed on top of the table. Now it's a test of nerve and blind luck – the player to the left of dealer must guess whether the next coin will be **'heads'** or **'tails'**. The top coin is then removed – if the player is correct, he/she then moves swiftly on to try and guess the orientation of the next coin. If wrong, the player simply drinks a two-finger/sip fine and continues to the next coin. When the player has worked through all of the remaining coins, drinking or surviving (depending on how lucky they are), the coins then move on to the next player who becomes the dealer, 'shuffles' the coins and then stacks them up as before.

Variants: More coins equals more chances to drink. Similar to the card-based **Landmine** game.

Hints & Tips
Obviously anyone clumsy enough to knock the coins over has to drink a penalty. 11 fingers should be a deterrent.

Bolloxed factor...

SPIN THE PENNY

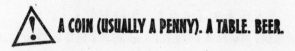

⚠ A COIN (USUALLY A PENNY). A TABLE. BEER.

ESSENTIAL SUPPLIES
A game of no skill whatsoever. But then they're usually the most effective...

Another effective, remarkably simple drinking game that's short on rules and big on drunken hilarity. Here's the gist: one player flips a coin, the player to the coin-flipper's immediate left guesses whether it will land on **'heads'** or **'tails'**. If the player manages to guess the result correctly, then he/she takes the coin from the first flipper and tosses it expertly for the player next to them (and so on around the group). If, however, somebody gets the guess wrong, then the player who chucked the coin spins it on the table and the unlucky player has to drink from his/her glass for as long as the coin keeps spinning. Then, just before it starts to settle, someone quickly smacks the spinning coin down on the table underneath their hand, and asks the bad-guesser to plump for heads and tails again. If he/she gets it right this time, the coin is passed on. But if he/she gets it wrong again, the coin is spun yet again and the same drinking penalty applies. Repeat until they get it right.

Hints & Tips
Be careful of your glasses when arresting the motion of the spinning coin. A separate table is recommended for the beer.

Bolloxed factor...
🍾🍾🍾🍾🍾🍾🍾

ANCHORMAN

⚠ **A TEAM GAME FOR BACKSTABBING INDIVIDUALS EVERYWHERE.**

ESSENTIAL SUPPLIES
**One coin per player. A table (with at least 2 feet of clearance).
A large jug of beer.**

nchorman is a simple team game (of some considerable skill) that can not only create a fierce rivalry between the people playing against each other, but amongst players on the same team. The game requires that at least eight people take part, or failing that, there must be an even number of potential coin-flickers and drinkers. Obviously, the more players you have in your drunken throng, the more dangerous it gets.

Here's how things work: two teams (of equal numbers) sit on opposite sides of a table and attempt, by flicking their coins, to get them into the large jug of beer. Each team member takes it in turn to shoot their coin towards the Jug-O-Beer, trying to make it land with a satisfying 'splunk' in the middle. Each player only shoots once per turn (even if they are successful in looping their coinage into the jug). When everyone on the team has flicked, the second team tries their luck with their own coins.

This continues until one team manages to get all of its complement of coins into the jug. The losing team then has to drink the jug of beer between them.

But here's the twist – before the losers drink, the winning team must choose someone to be the **"Anchorman"**. It's the **Anchorman's** job

64

Hints & Tips

If you get a draw (0-0 can become common at the end of the night) play again without drinking – you obviously all need to sober up a bit.

to drink last and to finish any remaining beer. Therefore the **Anchorman's** teammates can be as kind (everybody drinks in equal measures) or as nasty (everyone else takes a few mouthfuls and cruelly leaves the anchor to drain the rest) as they wish. While drinking the contents of the jug, the **Anchorman's** teammates cannot take their lips off it. If they do, even for a moment, they must pass the jug onto the next player. When the jug reaches the **Anchorman,** he/she has two minutes to drink the rest of the beer. When it's empty, simply refill the legendary Jug-O-Beer and begin anew.

Bolloxed factor...

CHEERS!

PENNY RUGBY

 AN ALCOHOL-TINGED VERSION OF AN INNOCENT OLD SCHOOL GAME.

ESSENTIAL SUPPLIES
A coin. A table. Beer. 2 players.

 classic, easy game of some skill with a fresh, slightly dangerous beer-related twist, **Penny Rugby** takes most of the pain out of its more physical namesake and replaces it with liberal doses of liquid anaesthesia.

Here's how it works: the two players sit opposite each other at a table. Using the width of a table, place a suitable coin (a 2-pence piece seems to work the best) on the edge so that it hangs half-over the lip of the table. Then, kick off this metal 'ball' by hitting the coin with your flattened palm so that it skids across the table. The idea behind the game is to then nudge the coin with your forefinger so that it skids further across the table and onto the opposite edge. You get three nudges after the initial kick off, with the ultimate objective being to nudge the coin so it hangs precariously over the other lip of the table

If after three nudges the coin is (a) still on the table because you haven't nudged it hard enough, or (b) somewhere on the floor because you've nudged it too hard, player two gets to have his/her turn, kicking off as before. If during your three nudges, you manage to manoeuvre the coin onto the opposite edge of the table, you can then attempt to score. To score a **try,** reach under the hanging coin with your forefinger and flip it into the air, attempting to catch it with the other hand. If you succeed, you score five points and can go for the conversion. If not, you fumble the ball at the last minute, score nothing

Hints & Tips
If you find you drink faster when NOT playing this game, just add some penalties for not getting into a try-scoring position after three nudges.

and drink a forfeit for your sheer cack-handedness. For the **conversion,** the opposing player forms a makeshift set of goalposts by pressing his/her two forefingers on the table, joining the thumbs together and raising them up like a set of posts. All the conversion-taker has to do is spin the coin on the table and catch it between his/her two thumbs. If caught successfully, the coin can then be flicked (still between the two thumbs) over player two's hand-made goalposts. Each time you score, the opposing player drinks. And vice versa.

Bolloxed factor...

PENNY FOOTBALL

 AN ALCOHOL-TINGED VERSION OF ANOTHER INNOCENT OLD SCHOOL GAME.

ESSENTIAL SUPPLIES
Three coins (two 2-pence pieces and a 1-pence piece). A table. Beer. 2 players.

ike **Penny Rugby** on the previous page, **Penny Football** involves skidding coins around on a tabletop. This time in a rudimentary simulation of England's greatest contribution to the culture and civilization of our planet.

Here's how it works: Once again, the two players sit opposite each other at a table. Using the width of a table, place the three coins on the edge so that one of the 2-pence pieces overhangs the table and the two remaining coins sit in front of it, each one touching the precariously-placed 2-pence (the three coins should form an inverted triangle shape).

Then, kick off this metallic trio by hitting the overhanging coin with your flattened palm so that the three coins fan out and skid across the table. Meanwhile, the second player closes his fist and extends both the forefinger and the little finger to make a goal (this is then placed on the table, two fingers on top, knuckles of the clenched fist resting against the edge).

What the attacking player has to do is to manoeuvre the 1-pence piece (the ball), by nudging it through the gap between the two 2-pence

68

Hints & Tips
If you want to drink more, try giving each player three turns and then having a penalty shoot-out if there's a draw.

pieces (the players), into a position where it can be nudged (again this must be through the two 2-pence pieces) into the opposing goal. Drink whenever the other player scores against you. The coins eventually pass to the opposing player when (a) a goal has been scored, (b) if the attacking player fails to move the 1-pence through the two 2-pence pieces, or (c) if the attacking players shot misses the goal. And no, you can't score with a 2-pence piece.

Bolloxed factor...

CHEERS!

BASEBALL

⚠️ **THEY SAY THAT PLAYING SPORT IS GOOD FOR YOU.
BUT NOT THIS VERSION OF BASEBALL...**

ESSENTIAL SUPPLIES
Four shot glasses. Beer. A coin. Some matchsticks. Two teams of people.

 lthough you might expect to see shot glasses arranged in a typical baseball diamond for this game, **Baseball** merely uses the idea of the popular US sport for shallow, alcoholic ends. Something to be heartily condoned, you'll surely agree.

In short: The four glasses are set up in a row moving away from the player. The nearest glass is the 'home base', the second is the 'first' and so on. One by one, each player in the team must step up to 'bat', i.e. they must attempt to flick a coin into any of the four shot glasses. Like baseball, the farther you can flick the coin, the better.

The first glass represents a single dash, the second a double, the third a triple, and the last a crowd-pleasing home run. Three strikes (if you manage to misses all four shot glasses) and you're out. Three outs by people on your team, and your innings is over and the other team steps up to bat.

The game runs along similar lines to baseball (or rounders if you can remember the rules from your schooldays) and runs are scored in the same way. If, for example, a player manages to flick a coin into the second shot glass, then their go ends and a matchstick is placed next to the glass denoting how far that player has managed to 'run' around the four bases. The player must then drink the contents of every shot

Hints & Tips
Patience is the key to this game. Aim low and keep the matchsticks moving. You won't drink too much, and your opponents will.

glass up to and including the glass that his/her coin landed in (in this case, the player would drink the home and the first base glasses. The glasses are then refilled and the next player steps up to flick a coin. If that player manages to flick it into the third glass, the matchstick on second base moves to the fourth glass, another one is placed on third, and the player drinks three shots.

Every time a matchstick manages to move onwards from the last glass, the batting team scores a **run** and the opposing team must take a drink. Anybody who **strikes out** (i.e. misses the glasses with their three attempts) must drink the contents of all four shot glasses.

Bolloxed factor...

TAPS

 IT MAY SOUND SIMPLE. BUT TAPS REQUIRES CONCENTRATION, FOCUS AND GOOD COORDINATION.

ESSENTIAL SUPPLIES
A coin. A table. Some beer.

 simple game with the bare minimum of verbal communication between players, **Taps** is less a game about shiny bathroom fittings, more a game of skill and dexterity that involves banging a coin on a table.

In this unspoken, fast-paced game, one player starts by tapping his/her coin once. The person sat immediately to the coin-tapper's left then taps his/her coin once and the process continues around the table. Tapping the coin once on the table maintains the current direction of the play. Tapping the coin twice reverses the direction (i.e. from left-to-right, from right-to-left), while tapping the coin quickly three times skips the next player. Play this game as quickly as possible. Anybody who misses a tap, or gets a tap wrong (banging the table when the direction of play has, in fact, been reversed; or tapping without realising that the player next to them has tapped three times, for instance), must drink the usual beer-related penalty.

 Hints & Tips
Watch your grandad's antique coffee table when you're playing this one; there'll be marks left.

Bolloxed factor...

SPOOF

⚠ **THE CLASSIC COIN GAME. PASSPORT TO DRUNKENNESS AND SPOONS OF LIME PICKLE.**

ESSENTIAL SUPPLIES
Three coins each. A curry house location. Beer. (Optional: lime pickle.)

Let's hear it for the traditional curry house party game – a game of skill, of extreme backstabbing, cunning, and of large drunkenness coupled with compulsory swallowing of lime pickle. Simply pick your favourite curry location, stock up with beer and make sure that each player has three coins with which to play the game. **It works thus:** each player puts their hands underneath the table and secretly puts either three, two, one or no coins at all into one hand. This clenched hand is then held over the table and the participating players take it in turns to guess the total number of coins held by all the players (if six people play, that's a maximum of 18 coins and a minimum of zero). When all of the guesses have been made, the players open their hands to reveal the coins inside. All the coins are totalled up and any player that has guessed the total correctly, wins the round and gets to sit out the remainder of the game. With the numbers whittled down a notch, the coin-hiding process begins again. Whichever player is left at the end of the game, having guessed each coin total incorrectly, has to drink a pint in one go and eat a generous spoonful of lime pickle.

Hints & Tips
You can also play this game in any bar to settle who has to pay to get the next round in. And fetch them. And buy nuts.

Bolloxed factor...
🍾🍾🍾🍾🍾🍾🍾🍾🍾

BOUNCE 'EM

⚠️ THE QUINTESSENTIAL DRINKING GAME. PORTABLE. EASY. DEADLY.

ESSENTIAL SUPPLIES
A coin. A cup/glass. A table. Beer.

On the one hand, **Bounce 'Em** is a game involving skill and luck, not to mention some keen dexterity, a touch of physics and an appreciation of the relationship between velocity and angles. And on the other, it's a game about throwing a coin against a table and bouncing it into a cup. Whichever you prefer.

Gather a group of friends around a table (six players is a good number) and decide who will go first – an easy way to do this is to spin the coin you'll be bouncing, say a light 5-pence piece, and whoever the Queen's nose points at (or the thistle's crown) gets to start the game. The aim of **Bounce 'Em** is simple and rather obvious – each player attempts to bounce a coin off of the table and into a glass or cup of beer. If the coin misses, the next player steps up to try his/her luck. But if it makes it in, the successful bouncer can pick one of the other players to drink a beer forfeit. Shoot successfully three times and you can then make up your own foolhardy rules.

Variants:
Bounce 'Em, Drink 'Em: How about this? The glass that you bounce the coin into is also the glass that contains the beer forfeit. The extra element of danger is trying to drink the beer without swallowing the coin that's swishing around in the bottom of the glass. Players who bounce hopeful coins which hit the rim of the glass ('oooh') and narrowly miss going in ('awww'), get another go for free. If a player

Hints & Tips

We've found that aiming the coin vertically at the table is the most effective method of getting a decent height on your bounce.

misses, but he feels confident that he/she will get the coin in 'the next time', the other players can encourage the player to 'chance their arm'. This means that the player is allowed one free attempt and, if the go succeeds the game continues as normal. If the chancy attempt fails, however, the unfortunate coin-shooter must drink all of the beer in the forfeit glass.

Ice Cube Bounce 'em: In short, instead of a cup, **Ice Cube Bounce 'Em** makes use of an ice cube tray, preferably one with two distinct sides. Play obviously continues as in the original **Bounce 'Em** game, only this time the coin is aimed at the empty tray. One half of the tray is designated the 'give' side (where drinking forfeits are dished out to the other participating players), while the other is the 'take' side (the shooter must drain the beer themselves like a L-O-S-E-R.) Make it more interesting by shooting your coins from further away each time. Or how about trying to bounce the coins off of two tables...?

Speed Bounce 'Em: Said to be more fun than the original game, **Speed Bounce 'Em** is played at three, four, even five times the pace of your basic **Bounce' Em** contest. That means no concentrating, no calculating flight paths, no thinking, no abortive attempts, just simply aim, fire, and miss. If you hesitate, you drink. It's as simple as that.

Bounce 'Em 2: Sit everybody in a circle. Give a coin each to two

people sitting opposite each other. Then, quite obviously, each player attempts to bounce their coin into the same glass (this time it's an empty one). The players get as many attempts as they want and, when one of the players does finally get a coin to clink into the glass, the successful person retrieves said coin and passes it on to the person sitting on their left. This process continues until somebody in the circle gets passed a coin when they already have a coin that they're trying to launch into the glass. This person is then mocked mercilessly and forced to drink an entire pint. Very, very quickly.

Bolloxed factor...

DROP THE PENNY

⚠ **THINK JENGA, BUCKAROO, KERPLUNK OR CARD PYRAMIDS. BUT WITH A NAPKIN AND A FAG.**

ESSENTIAL SUPPLIES
A cigarette. A glass. A paper napkin. A coin. Beer.

Remember the old kids game **Jaws**? A game where you had to hook plastic debris out of a big shark's mouth before it snapped shut...? Or how about **Kerplunk**? The old family favourite involving a clear plastic cylinder, straws and a bag of marbles...? Well, **Drop The Penny** is similar to both of them. Only it involves burning away a napkin with an unhealthy fag.

To play, get a paper napkin, place it across a glass and place a light coin on top of it – say a 5-pence piece. The aim is a simple one: how much of the napkin can you burn away (taking turns, each player MUST make a discernible hole) without causing the structural integrity of the napkin to fail and the coin to drop? Whoever burns too much of the napkin away, and makes the coin drop into the glass, is announced as the loser and must drink a whole pint of beer as a punishment and get the next round in.

Hints & Tips
In the early stages of the game it can be a good idea to burn big holes, speeding the game up considerably.

Bolloxed factor...

CHANDELIERS

 A GAME LIKE BOUNCE 'EM. NOTHING TO DO WITH ORNATE LIGHTING FIXTURES.

ESSENTIAL SUPPLIES
A large glass or jug. Some smaller glasses. A table. Beer.

This is a game that's quite a lot ike **Bounce 'Em** (see page 73), but **Chandeliers** differs in several key areas. For starters, it moves a lot faster and this is mainly due to the fact that there are more targets to hit – specifically a large glass of beer in the middle of the table and a ring of smaller glasses surrounding it.

Here's how it works: A large glass (say, a pint glass) is topped up with beer and placed in the middle of the table. Some smaller glasses (half-pint tumblers, enough of them for each player) are also filled with alcohol, probably some sort of appropriate short, and these are then positioned around the large centre glass in front of the other players in the circle.

One by one, the players try to bounce their coins at the glasses as before, hoping to hit either the small glasses or the big pint glass. If the coin lands in one of the smaller glasses, the player sitting nearest the glass must drink the contents and refill the glass with beer.

If the coin lands in the large glass, all of the players around the table have to drink the booze in the glasses next to them. The last player to slam their empty glass down on the table is deemed the **'loser'** and must subsequently drink the beer in the pint glass as a penalty (Note of caution: As with any 'slamming' activity, make sure the glasses are of the thick, durable type. There's nothing more irritating than a lengthy

Hints & Tips
You can stand where you like when bouncing the coin, so don't throw on the side with your glass. The pint then forms a handy shield.

trip to your local Accident & Emergency Department in the middle of an exciting and frenzied drinking game. It tends to disrupt the flow.)

After this bout of nervous excitement, all the glasses are refilled and the coin passes to the next player. Repeat the game until drowsy. If the room starts spinning, it's probably a good idea to give up. You've gone too far.

Bolloxed factor...

CHAPTER 3

DICE GAMES

Like cards, money and TV programmes, the use of dice in a drinking game is principally to generate that random element that keeps the competition exciting. Unlike more rigidly-structured pub and word games that rely on a constant degree of concentration, card-, money-, and dice-based games are great levellers. So you don't have to be good at thinking of celebrity names or at throwing coins into strategically-placed ice cube trays. Playing with dice randomises the dangers and the drinking penalties, creating drinking entertainment where the only thing you can rely on is faith and a large helping of blind luck. In the pages that follow, we've collected the 16 best dice games known to mankind, a jamboree bag of dice-based mania that ranges from the simple (**Just Dice**) to the more involved (**Bunko**), taking in the wildly imaginative (**Dice Man**) and the seemingly stupid (**Boxhead**) along the way. And all you need are a couple of those familiar numbered cubes...

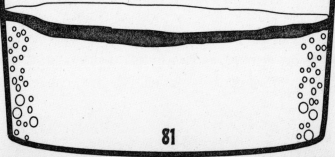

CHEAT DICE

 A SLOW-STARTER, BUT THIS GAME IS AN ADDICTIVE BLEND OF TRUTH AND DARE.

ESSENTIAL SUPPLIES

Five dice. A table. Beer. The ability to lie, cheat and scheme.

 ll you have to do is lay your hands on five dice. That'll be enough for you to enjoy the drinking game **Cheat Dice**; an irresistible mix of luck and bare-faced cheek. Like its card-based variant, **Cheat**, the rules are simple.

Player one rolls the five dice (WITHOUT letting the other players see how they land) and, leaving the dice hidden on the table, announces the result. He/she may, of course, 'cheat' and lie about the result. The other players must then decide whether they believe the player is telling the truth, i.e. whether he/she has actually thrown three 4s, a 2 and a 1 or if his/her roll is actually lower and far less impressive.

If the first player is believed, the next player takes his/her turn to roll the dice, aiming to score a higher total (see **Scoring**) than the previous dice-tumbler. Again, he/she should roll the dice WITHOUT letting the other players see the result. And, naturally enough, he/she has the option to 'cheat'. If the total is not higher, the player must drink a forfeit (decided by the playing group beforehand). However, if at any time another player believes that the dice-chucker is lying about their score, he/she may challenge the total by shouting **'Cheat'**. The player in control of the dice must then reveal the true roll. If his/her claim is false, the dice-rolling player must drink a forfeit. If the claim is true, the challenging player must drink the forfeit. Play then passes on to the next player.

Hints & Tips
If you always lose money at Poker, don't try playing this game. Unless, that is, you WANT to get so drunk you can't even fall over properly.

Scoring Cheat Dice: Five Of A Kind beats Four Of A Kind beats A Full House (i.e. three 4s and two 3s) beats Three Of A Kind beats a Pair. Naturally, five 6s beat five 5s, five 4s and so on.

Variant: You can change this game most easily by adding to the number of throws allowed. Players may re-roll as many dice as they like up to, say, three times. A more twisted variant is **Cumulative Cheat Dice**. In this game each player gets one roll more than the previous player to try and beat the last total. That's the good news. The bad news is that the forfeit is multiplied by the number of rolls allowed.

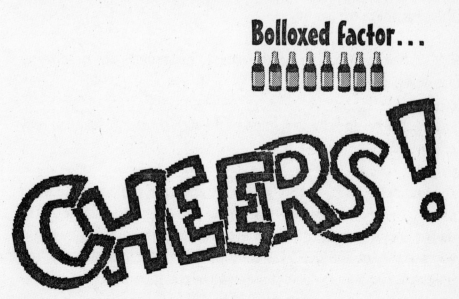

Bolloxed factor...

CHEERS!

83

DICE MAN

 EMBARKING ON A DICE MAN JOURNEY MIGHT BE THE BEST (AND LAST) THING YOU EVER DO...

ESSENTIAL SUPPLIES
One die. A wild imagination. The world...

 nspired by the cult novel of the same name (in which a man makes all the decisions in his life by simply assigning numbers to the options and rolling a dice), the **Dice Man** game is not only deadly, but immensely portable, variable and exciting.

The idea behind the game is simple, but highly effective. A player is nominated to be the proverbial **Dice Man** or **Woman** and the only rule he/she has to observe is that the **Dice Man** MUST abide by the law of the die. He/she rolls a dice, and away you go.

The laws of the die are thus:

The '1' shall always mean that the die is to be immediately passed onto the next player.

The '6' shall be an action invented by the dice-chucker (usually an easy one, obviously)

The numbers '2', '3', '4' and '5' shall be actions invented by the other players. These actions or tasks can be anything – buy the next round of drinks, chat a girl up in the corner, chat a guy up in the corner, spill someone's pint and get away with it, steal someone's pint, etc. The only limit is your imagination (tempered by a certain degree of morality and ethics, although don't go too far: 'Tidy up your room' is hardly

Hints & Tips
Don't pick actions that are too difficult. The dice-chucker will go for a drink forfeit AND remember your unkindness when it's your throw.

going to lead to an action-packed drinking night to remember) and a desire to obey the will of the die. So if the action for '3' is catch a train to Glasgow, you should do exactly that. If the die comes to a stop on a '2' (leave the pub and go for a curry) then the die should be obeyed.

The actions shall be assigned BEFORE the dice are rolled.

Anyone who fails to obey the die, is subject to a drinking penalty. Let's say a pint. Downed in less than a minute.

Bolloxed factor...

DROP DEAD

 A TWISTED, BEER-SOAKED GAME SIMILAR TO YAHTZEE. BUT WITH BEER.

ESSENTIAL SUPPLIES
Five dice. A table. Beer.

ike **Cheat Dice, Drop Dead** involves throwing five dice to amass the highest total possible. Play is taken in turn, and if there are a lot of you it's a good idea to get pen and paper from behind the bar so that you can keep track of the scores.

Each player throws the dice and then adds up the total. As long as the numbers '2' and '5' are not part of the roll's total, the player can collect the dice up again and roll anew, adding the subsequent score (again, unless there is a '2' or a '5' in the roll) to the first score. The player can continue, taking a drink between each roll, until either of the two bogey numbers appear.

If a '**2**' is thrown then the unfortunate player scores a big fat zero for the roll and the dice that showed the '2' are left out from the next roll.

Likewise, if a player reveals a '**5**' in his roll, the score doesn't count and the dice that showed the number is also excluded.

For example, if a player throws three 6s, a 3 and a 1 on his first roll, he can boast a total of 22. If on the second roll the dice reveal two 4s, one 3 and two 2s, the player doesn't score any additional points. Having faltered with two 2s, these dice are removed from play and on the next roll only three dice can be used.

Hints & Tips
If you can find a table that adjoins a wall, much fun can be had rolling your dice 'Craps' style with forfeits for any that fall off.

Play continues like this, with the player drinking between each dice roll, until a '5' or a '2' is rolled on the last die. When this happens, the player's turn ends, the score is totalled up and control of the dice passes onto the next player. The winner is the player with the highest total after two rounds of play, and he/she can laugh while the losers drink a suitable forfeit.

Bolloxed factor...

THREE MAN

 THE DRINKING GAME EQUIVALENT OF "YOU'RE IT".

ESSENTIAL SUPPLIES
Two dice. A table. Beer.

ather a group of players together, and let everybody roll the two dice until one player reveals a '3'. When this happens, the player who rolled '3' becomes the **'Three Man'** and the game can begin.

Each player in the group rolls the two dice in turn, whereupon the gathered players must quickly add up the total on the two spotted cubes and perform the relevant action/task (as detailed below). The last person to compete the specified action must drink a forfeit – i.e. two fingers/sips, half-a-pint, etc. If, however, somebody rolls a **three** (in total) then the **Three Man** must drink a four-finger/sip or some similar nasty forfeit. As for the dicey tasks that have to be performed, they are as follows:

If the dice show **'1' & '3'**: everyone touches their glass to edge of the table. The last one to do this incurs the usual drinking forfeit (say, two fingers/sips from their pint) If the dice show **'1' & '4'**: everyone puts their thumb on their forehead. The last one to do so incurs the drinking forfeit. If the dice show **'1' & '5'**: a social drink, everyone drains some beer from their glasses. If the dice total **'7'**: the person to the right of dice-chucker takes a penalty drink. If the dice total **'11'**: the person to left of dice-roller takes a penalty drink. If the dice roll is **a double**: the dice-flicker adds up the total number of spots on the dice and gives that many penalties away to the rest of the group. Apart from the **Three**

Hints & Tips

Keep a particularly close eye out for the '1 & 3' and the '1 & 4'. A little alertness will save you from a lot of grief.

Man. If the penalty is given to the **Three Man** by mistake, then the current dice-roller becomes the new **Three Man.** If the dice roll off table: the dice-roller incurs a drinking penalty for his carelessness. If someone spills their drink: the guilty party incurs a drinking penalty for their lack of coordination.

Note: any dice roll not listed here is to be considered a "null" or "dead" roll, causing the dice to be passed onto the next player.

BOXHEAD

 A SIMPLE, EFFECTIVE GAME OF CHANCE PLAYED WITH UNUSUAL HEADGEAR.

ESSENTIAL SUPPLIES
Two dice. An empty cardboard box. Beer. Spirits.

Developed, so it is said, at the University of Victoria in Canada, the **Boxhead** drinking game is loosely based on the old **Three Man** game that you should now be familiar with. Like most drinking games, it's easy-to-pick up, yet the random nature of the game makes it impossible to master. Gather your players around a large table, nominate somebody to go first and then roll the two dice in turn, noting the result and applying the rules listed below.

If the dice **total '2'**: everybody takes a drink (usual penalty of two fingers/sips) If the dice **total '3'**: the person sitting to the left of the dice-roller drinks. If the dice **total '4'**: nothing happens. Move onto the next player. If the dice **total '5'**: roll another die. The result equals the number of fingers/sips everyone at the table must drink. If the dice **total '6'**: the dice-roller can make up a new rule. Further rolls of '6' will activate this new rule although the dice-roller can make up a new one afterwards if he/she wishes. If the dice **total '7'**: players slap their hands down on the table. The last one to do this drinks. If the dice **total '8'**: roll another die. The result equals the number of fingers/sips that are poured into a glass for the dice-roller to drink. If the dice **total '9'**: the person sitting to the right of the dice-roller drinks. If the dice **total '10'**: toilet break. Unless you can roll a '10' you won't be allowed to leave the table. If the dice **total '11' or '12'**: **Boxhead!** The dice-roller must wear the cardboard box on their head (this is particularly effective in pubs) until he/she rolls another '11' or '12' to remove it. However, if

90

Hints & Tips

On no account hit the cardboard box while it is on someone's head. They won't know who's doing it and may become agitated.

another player rolls an '11' or '12', the box is automatically transferred to them. And, worse than the indignity of wearing a box on your noggin, the **Boxhead** must also drink whenever anybody else in the game drinks. With some difficulty, obviously.

Variations:

Double Boxhead: Unsurprisingly, you'll need two cardboard boxes for this version. **Double Boxhead** follows **Boxhead** rules to the letter, the only real difference being that there are two boxes in play. So, the first player to roll an '11' or '12' wears one box, the second player to do so gets the other one. The same rules apply to get rid of the box. Players cannot wear two boxes on their head (unless the boxes are different sizes and it is funny).

Oracle Boxhead Played in the same way as normal **Boxhead,** the difference here is that before each dice roll, you get to ask the **Boxhead** one question. Just as in the old party game **Truth Or Dare,** the wearer of the box must give a truthful answer to the question. If anybody at the table can prove that the **Boxhead** has lied, the wearer faces triple the usual drinking penalty.

Triple Death Boxhead: Imagine normal **Boxhead**, but played with THREE dice instead of two... Yet there aren't an extra six rules to add onto the 12 already covered in the original game. Instead, **Triple Death**

DICE GAMES

Boxhead dares you to carry out all possible combinations of the three dice rolled. For example, if a player rolls a '3', a '6' and a '2', all of the following actions apply: 3+6=9 (the person sitting to the right of the dice-roller drinks); 3+2=5 (roll another die. The result equals the number of fingers/sips everyone at the table must drink); 6+2=8 (roll another die. The result equals the number of fingers/sips that are poured into a glass for the dice-roller to drink). Three times the fun...

Pinball Boxhead Every time a player finishes a drink, he/she should place the empty cup/glass/can in front them on the table. After a while, each player should have built up a sizeable wall of empties. With these walls in place, the dice are rolled one at a time... The only thing is, the aim now is to bounce the dice off of the other players walls, just like a pinball bouncing around a table. If you manage to bounce it off two walls, you can double the eventual penalty. Off three walls, then triple it. When both dice have landed, the usual **Boxhead** rules apply, modified by the pinball bonus. Note: if the dice should leave the table at any time during an enthusiastic throw, the dice-roller concerned must finish his beer in one go.

Bolloxed factor...

MAGIC DICE

ANOTHER RANDOM DRINK-A-THON, AND PERFECT FOR LOUDMOUTHS EVERYWHERE.

ESSENTIAL SUPPLIES
One die per player. A table. Beer.

Before every round of **Magic Dice,** pick a player to be the **'mouth'** and then give everybody in the group one die. The rules are simple – in a fit of choreographed recklessness, all of the players roll their dice onto the table simultaneously. At the same time, the designated **'mouth'** calls out a number between 1-6 and the players incur a forfeit (the usual two-fingers/sips will suffice) if the number yelled matches the spots shown on their tumbled dice. The **'mouth'** can also mix things up a bit by calling either **'even'** or **'odd'**, whereupon anybody who has an even or odd number on their dice, incurs **double** the usual penalty. There's an added risk, however, because if the **'mouth'** calls even and ends up with a '2', '4' or '6' showing on his/her own die, or calls odd and is unfortunate enough to get a '1', '3' or '5', he/she must drink **triple** the two-finger/sip penalty.

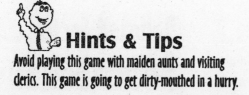

Hints & Tips
Avoid playing this game with maiden aunts and visiting clerics. This game is going to get dirty-mouthed in a hurry.

Bolloxed factor...

93

THRESHOLD

 HEADS OR TAILS? GUESS THE ORIENTATION OF THE COIN OR PAY THE LIQUID PENALTY.

ESSENTIAL SUPPLIES
A die. A cup. A coin. A table. Beer.

How simple can a game be? Even after seven pints of lager, a couple of gins and a curry, the rules for this game remain crystal clear and addictively simple. **(1)** Get a cup. **(2)** Put the dice and the coin in the cup. **(3)** Each player gets a chance to shake the contents of the cup and to ask the player next to them to guess whether the coin will land on 'heads' or 'tails'. **(4)** The shaker of the cup then empties the dice and the coin hopefully onto the tabletop, noting the orientation of the coin and the number shown on the dice. **(5)** If the guessing player gets the 'heads/tails' forecast correct, the shaker of the cup is forced to drink X fingers/sips of beer - where X is the number shown on the dice. **(6)** If the guessing player gets the 'heads/tails' forecast wrong, however, he/she must drink as many fingers/sips at the upturned die has spots.

Variations: Stupid Threshold Essentially the same as **Threshold,** but played with two coins.

Bloody Stupid Threshold: Essentially the same as **Stupid Threshold,** but played with two coins and two dice.

Hints & Tips
To avoid confusing yourself, write 'heads' or 'tails' clearly on a beermat in front of you and shout it when someone asks.

Bolloxed factor...

94

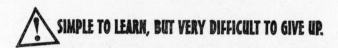

TWENTY-ONE ACRES

⚠ SIMPLE TO LEARN, BUT VERY DIFFICULT TO GIVE UP.

ESSENTIAL SUPPLIES
Five dice. Beer. Spirits.

Another tiny but effective game that's easy on a beer-addled brain and a breeze to learn. Unlike other dice games which count all of the numbers on a dice, **Twenty-One Acres** is only interested in the amount of '1's that are rolled by the participating players.

Here's how it works: each player takes it in turn to roll the five dice. If a '1' is rolled then the players either make a mental note of it or scribble it down on a handy piece of paper, beermat or cigarette packet. The player that rolls the seventh '1' of the game is the player who gets to pick what drink will be consumed later in the game (beer, vodka, gin, whatever your poison). The player who rolls the 14th '1' of the game is the player who gets to pay for the drink specified earlier. Finally the player who rolls the 21st '1' is the lucky soul who gets to drink the chosen (and now paid for) drink in one.

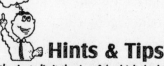

Hints & Tips
It's wise to limit the size of the drink that's picked, to avoid the evening becoming uncontrollably expensive.

Bolloxed factor...

BUNKO

⚠ A GAME FOR THE EARLY EVENING, WHEN PLAYERS CAN
STILL STRING THOUGHTS TOGETHER.

ESSENTIAL SUPPLIES
Six dice. Two tables. Eight players. Beer. Some paper. A pen.

 game that can only be played with groups of four people, **Bunko** is a slightly complex dice game that's played in rounds. Simply put, the aim of **Bunko** is for your team (two players) to amass 21 points before the opposing team (two players) does.

If there are eight players involved (that's two teams of four), these are split between two tables – two play two on table 1 and two play two on table 2. Team partners sit opposite each other and, rolling three dice in turn, each player tries to get as many '6's as possible. **Each 6** rolled is worth **one point,** and the player in control of the dice keeps rolling until none of the three dice rolled shows a six. When this happens, play passes to the next player on the opposing team, and so on around the table. The winners are the first partnership to make it to the magical 21 point total with their combined scores.

However, there are some finer points to the gameplay. Firstly, if a player rolls **three '1's** at any time, the team loses all their points – this is termed a **'wipeout'.** If a player manages to roll **three '6's**, the proverbial **'Bunko'**, the rolling player gets three points, while both teams get the chance to earn a bonus. Whenever a **Bunko** appears, the table becomes free and anyone, from either team, can try to pick up the dice from the table. Each dice recovered is worth an extra point – so if the **Bunko**-rolling team manage to retrieve all three dice, they get an extra three points to add to their score. But if the opposing team

Hints & Tips
You have to be poised to be quick off the mark when a 'Bunko' occurs.
This should be the responsibility of the non dice-thrower.

manage to grab the dice, they score the extra points despite the fact that it is not their go at the table. Winning partnerships then swap tables, playing the other team members.

And where exactly does the excessive drinking come in? Glad you asked. While **Bunko** can certainly be played for fun, a lot of the fun comes from adding an alcoholic element to the proceedings. For example, **'wipeouts'** (when a dice roll serves up three '1's) could also be punished with a drinking forfeit; **Bunko** rolls are given an extra edge by penalising the rolling team if they don't retrieve at least two of the three dice after a trio of sixes. Add to that the fact that you can make up penalties for most losses, most wipeouts, or if a team rolls three '2's, '3's, '4's or '5's. The possibilities are endless. Why not try a couple of games for yourself.

Bolloxed factor...

SIX PACK

 A FAST-PACED GAME OF GLASS-FILLING AND GLASS-EMPTYING.

ESSENTIAL SUPPLIES
Six glasses. Beer.

Arrange six glasses (half-pint tumblers for amateurs, pint-glasses for the pros) in a row and number them from 1-6. Half-fill glasses '1', '3' and '5' with beer and leave the others empty. Now take your trusty die, pick somebody to go first and begin as follows:

Each player rolls the die and, on seeing the result, picks up the corresponding glass. If it's **a full glass** then the player drinks the beer and then passes the die onto the person to his/her left. If it's **an empty glass,** the player is obliged to pour some of his own drink into it, before passing the die onto the next player. This process continues around the table until people are either (a) drunk. Or (b) annoyed that they've given away too much beer. Drunkenness or penniless sobriety rests on the throw of the die...

 Hints & Tips
This is a game that becomes much more fun if everybody's drinking something different. Variety is the spice, etc.

Bolloxed factor...

🍾🍾🍾🍾🍾🍾

JUST DICE

⚠️ **A RELATIVELY SIMPLE GAME. AS LONG AS YOU JOT DOWN THE STRING OF PENALTY RULES.**

ESSENTIAL SUPPLIES
Two dice. Beer. Spirits.

imilar to **Three Man, Just Dice** is a much simpler, quicker game, but still one that get you sloshed out of your brain in under two hours. The rules are straightforward – each player rolls two dice and notes the numbers that come up. Rolls that **add up to a '6'** (1&5, 2&4) or **have a '6'** in them (6&1, 6&2, 6&3, 6&4, 6&5), incurs the traditional beer-down-the-hatch penalty. In addition, rolling a **double '2', double '4'** or a **double '5',** incurs an X finger/sip penalty (where X is the number of the double thrown). A **double '3'** incurs two separate penalties, the usual two-finger/sip penalty for having two numbers that add up to '6', plus a three-finger/sip penalty for the double. Worse still, roll a **double '1'** or a **double '6'** and the player to your left gets to pour you a shot of your least favourite spirit. You, naturally, must down it in one.

Hints & Tips
When asked what your least favourite spirit is you MUST tell the truth. To do otherwise would be unprincipled. Ahem.

Bolloxed factor...

MEXICAN

 A GAME OF MEXICANS, SCUMBAGS AND POINT SCORING.

ESSENTIAL SUPPLIES
Two dice. A pen. Some paper. Beer.

Slightly more involved than most drinking games, **Mexican** can nevertheless lead to a long and competitive evening of drunkenness. Again, like **Three Man** and **Boxhead,** the game involves rolling two dice and performing the tasks (drink-related, of course) that are associated with them. In this case, however, **Mexican** is also about amassing a decent score over your opponents. Dice rolls are subject to the following punishments and penalties:

If the dice show **'1' & '2'**: this is called a **'Mexican'**, the lowest possible roll and so the most nasty. Every time a **Mexican** is thrown, the standard drink penalty (let's say, one finger/sip of beer) is doubled. If the dice show **'1' & '3'**: this is known as a **'Scumbag'**. The dice-roller must immediately finish his current drink, whether it's a quick shot of Tequila or a full pint of lager. If the dice show **a double**: the dice-thrower's score increases by the number of the double multiplied by 100. I.e. if a double '2' is thrown, the player's score increases by 2 x 100=200. **Any other throw**: another scoring roll. Simply take the highest number on the two dice and multiply it by 10 + the smallest number. I.e. 6&4 scores 64, 3&2 scores 32.

The player that starts the game has a choice of taking **up to three** rolls to get the highest score possible. However many you decide to take, the final score is always the total amassed on the last throw, whether it's the first, second or third attempt. Once the starting player has

Hints & Tips
There are enough Mexican games in this book to make a theme night:
Moustaches, stupid accents; the fun is probably endless.

decided on how many dice rolls he/she is going to make, the other players must follow suit. I.e. if the starting player decides to take only one dice roll, everybody else in the game can only take one roll too. However, the two dice do NOT have to be thrown at the same time. If a player has more than one throw available, he/she can elect to only roll one of the two dice the second time around. I.e. if a player has two throws available, and rolls a 5&1 on the first go, he/she may decide to only pick up the '5' and to throw that die again (thereby increasing the chances of a **Mexican** or a **Scumbag**). But, as the object of the game is to amass the highest score, the player may want to rethrow the '1' to increase the points total. The loser is the player who scores the lowest and so he must incur the penalty drink as a result.

Variations:
Mega-Mexican: For real masochism, try adding a third die; one that's a different colour to the two point-scoring dice. Thus, when drinking penalties occur, the player must not only drink the traditional finger/sip punishment (and this may have been increased by **Mexicans** during the game), but he/she must repeat the penalty X times (where X is the number on the third die).

Bolloxed factor...

MEXICO

 NO MEXICANS OR SCUMBAGS IN THIS DICE-BASED VARIANT OF CHEAT.

ESSENTIAL SUPPLIES
Two dice. A cup. A pen. Some paper. Beer.

s another version of the **Mexican** game, the unadventurously titled **Mexico** not only refines the rules, but makes the gameplay slightly more dangerous by introducing an element of bluff.

Again, **Mexico** revolves around the chucking of two dice onto a table, but this time the dice are rattled around in a cup which is slammed down on the table to hide the dice roll from the other players. The dice-roller is allowed to take a look at the result and, like **Mexican,** the highest number gets multiplied by 10 and added to the lower number. Rolling a '5' and a '6', for example, would give you a score of 64. But, as you always have to roll a bigger, better score than the previous player, you may have to lie about it. Dice rolls are ranked in the following order: 1&1; 2&1; other doubles (6&6, 5&5, etc.); 6&5; 6&4; 6&3; 6&2; 6&1 and so on.

Once the dice- rolling player has **announced** his score, he waits for somebody to challenge him or call him a **liar.** If nobody does, the roll stands and the dice move onto the next player. If, however, the dice-roller IS challenged, the challenger can lift up the cup to see if the dice-roller is telling the truth. If he/she was telling the truth, the challenger must drink half-a-pint of beer. If the dice-roller is proved to be a liar, he/she downs the penalty half.

Hints & Tips

Make sure you understand the ranking system of the different rolls before you start bluffing, otherwise you'll definitely come a cropper.

Special rules apply for rolls of **1&1** (tell any opponent to drink half-a-pint... if they **don't believe you** but you have rolled a true 1&1, this penalty is **doubled**) and rolls of **1&2** (which changes the direction in which the dice are passed around the table).

Extra rules: if you drop a die (and someone notices), drink one finger/sip. If you drop both dice, drink two fingers/sips. If you slam the cup down on the table and one die sneaks out, drink one finger/sip. If you lose a die, drink a whole pint.

Bolloxed factor...

SPEED DICE

 **⚠ ROLL THE DICE, DRINK THE BEER. WHAT COULD BE SIMPLER?**

ESSENTIAL SUPPLIES
Two dice. Beer.

Short and sweet, all you need for a passport to oblivion is a pair of dice and a table to chuck them on to. Everybody in the group rolls two dice and adds up their score. The loser is the player with the lowest combined score from the two dice and must drink the **difference** between the highest score and the lowest score in fingers/sips. If there is a tie for the lowest score, both losers must drink the hefty forfeit.

Variations:
If any player rolls a **six,** they get to roll that die again adding the extra number to the total. Larger totals = bigger differences. And ultimately this means **more drinking.**

 **Hints & Tips**
The only advice we can offer when playing this game is to wear a helmet. It'll help when you fall over.

Bolloxed factor...

104

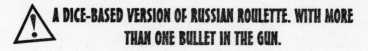

FORFEIT DICE

⚠ **A DICE-BASED VERSION OF RUSSIAN ROULETTE. WITH MORE THAN ONE BULLET IN THE GUN.**

ESSENTIAL SUPPLIES
Three dice. A table. Beer.

Before play starts, take some time out to decide on six individual forfeits (i.e. drinking two fingers/sips of beer, downing your pint, buying the next round, etc.) and to **assign each** one a number from **1-6**. Set one of the three dice aside – this will be known as the **'forfeit die'** and will be used to decide which one of the six penalties you have created will be applied to losing players. Now for the game itself – each player in turn takes the two remaining dice and rolls them in full view of the other players. The next player must then guess whether his dice-roll will have a higher total than the previous players. When he/she has plumped for **'higher'** or **'lower'**, the dice are rolled and result examined. If the player is right, then he/she gets to roll the dice for a second time, again guessing whether the total will be **'higher'** or **'lower'** than the first. If the player is correct again, then play passes onto the next player in the group. **Two correct guesses** in a row and **play passes** onto the next player in the group. If, however, a dice-rolling player gets two guesses wrong back-to-back, then he/she must pay a forfeit which is decided randomly by rolling the **'forfeit die'**.

Hints & Tips
Students of odds will tell you that a '7' is the most common total with two dice. That may help you.

Bolloxed factor...

105

7-11-DOUBLES

⚠️ **A FAST-PACED GAME WITH LOTS OF BOOZE THAT REQUIRES A MINIMUM OF BRAINPOWER.**

ESSENTIAL SUPPLIES
Two dice. A table. An empty pint glass. Beer.

Another simple dice game, heavily laced with the possibility of extreme drunkenness. Each player takes two dice and rolls them, taking careful note of the result. If the dice-chucker comes up with a **7**, an **11**, or any **double,** then he can pick somebody at random to drink a forfeit.

The forfeit: Whoever is chosen must first locate the empty pint glass (making sure NOT to touch it with their hands) and then fill it half-full with beer.

The aim of the game, is for the forfeiting player to drink the contents of the pint glass BEFORE the player with the dice manages to roll another **'7', '11' or double**. The player with the dice cannot roll them until the forfeiting player has **touched** the pint glass.

If the forfeiting player manages to drink the beer in the glass before the dice show any of the relevant bogey numbers, then play passes onto the next player. If, however, the forfeiting player does not manage to drain the amount of penalty booze before a **'7', '11' or double** is rolled, then another half of beer is added to the glass and the process begins again. This continues until the player beats the dice-roller.

Note: Any form of abuse of the dice by anybody involved with the game – throwing them wildly off of the table, clattering them into other

Hints & Tips

If you have to pay the forfeit, make sure you've got everything planned BEFORE you touch the pint glass. Or suffer the consequences.

people's drinks, seeing if you can bounce them down the corridor and through the toilet doors – incurs a **hefty** one-pint penalty.

Also note: if the penalty beer glass is ever filled, a fresh glass shall be sought out and the excess penalty deposited therein.

Bolloxed factor...

CHEERS!

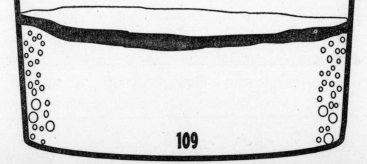

CHAPTER 4

MISCELLANEOUS GAMES

They're the games that don't seem to fit in anywhere else. Games that don't need dice, cash, a TV or cards, just an open mind and rock-hard drinking stamina. What they might need, however, are things like matchboxes, beer mats, empty bottles, pool tables or dart boards. They're easy to pick up, addictive to play and immensely satisfying (as long as you're not the dribbling, hazy-headed loser at the end of the evening). So indulge yourselves in 22 of the finest gaming miscellany ever assembled. Slap the table in **Chain Reaction;** play **Killer Pool;** toss plastic goblets in **Turbo Cups;** or, if you happen across a length of 20ft bungee cord, kill a couple of hours (and a few hundred brain cells) with the rarely-seen **Beer Bungee** game. As for **Beat The Barman,** if you've got the balls for it, we salute you. However, we do not condone theft of any kind and injuries received by enthusiastic drinkers are their own business.

CHAIN REACTION

⚠ **LIKE 'RUB YOUR BELLY, TAP YOUR HEAD AT THE SAME TIME', BUT SLIGHTLY DIFFERENT.**

ESSENTIAL SUPPLIES
Beer. Good coordination.

The drinking, unthinking man's equivalent to the children's game of 'rub your belly, tap your head at the same time', **Chain Reaction** becomes hysterically funny the more you lose at it. And to be honest, losing is pretty easy. Not bad for a game that doesn't feature dice, cards, cash, cups, matchboxes, tongue-twisting words or props of any kind.

All that you need to do to play **Chain Reaction** is to huddle together in a circle (or in a line along the bar) and to place both hands out in front of you so that they are resting, palms-down, on a flat surface. Now, cross your arms so that your left hand rests on the table to the right and the right hand rests on the left. Spread them apart a bit further so that your left hand is in front of the person to your right and your right hand is in front of the person to your left.

Make sure the rest of the group follow this process otherwise you'll get some strange looks from the barstaff. Actually, you'll get those anyway, so if that's going to put you off, you'd better not play this. When everybody is in position, with their hands in front of the people next to them, all you need to start a **Chain Reaction** is for someone to slap the table. Then, what should ideally happen is that a slapping wave

Hints & Tips

Obviously the more people you can get to join in with this, the more fun it's going to be. This is a great game for stag nights or weddings.

should ripple around the circle (or down the line) as each person slaps down their hands in sequence. Anybody who fails to move their hand at the right time, or moves it at the wrong time, must drink the usual forfeit. If you're playing this in a line, instead of a circle, you'll have to decide whether you want the chain to rebound, or wrap around when it comes to the end.

Bolloxed factor...

CHEERS!

THE MATCHBOX GAME

⚠ **YOU'VE FLIPPED COINS, CUPS AND DICE. SO WHY NOT A MATCHBOX?**

ESSENTIAL SUPPLIES
One full matchbox. A table. An empty pint glass. Beer.

 ather your drinking group around a suitable table and make sure everybody has a full drink in front of them. Pester a chain-smoker for a box of matches and then nominate a player to go first. Getting started is easy.

The idea of the game is to hold the matchbox below the level of the table and then to throw it up in the air so that it lands, in one of several different positions, on top of the table. Each player in the group gets a go at this in turn, facing the drink-related consequences when the matchbox lands:

If the box lands on its **long side,** there is a two-finger/sip penalty.

If the box lands on its **short side,** the penalty is four fingers/sips.

But whoever threw the box doesn't necessarily have to drink the penalty, that only happens when the box lands face up or face down. If it lands on edge, the thrower is safe and the next person must have a go. The penalties accumulate until the box lands **face-up** or **face-down,** whereupon the current box-hurler is lumbered with a BIG fine.

Hints & Tips

This is another game where practice makes perfect. It is quite possible to control the edge on which the box lands, you just have to know how.

Variants:

The **DIY Matchbox Game**. Again, everybody sits around the table with full drinks and the idea is the same – to chuck the matchbox from below the table to land on top of it. The difference in this **DIY** version is that by adding an empty pint glass to the table, you create a new angle to the game. The glass becomes the **'rules' glass,** and if a player manages to launch the matchbox from underneath the table to land **in the glass,** he/she can make up a new rule to spice up the gameplay. Confident players might even like to attempt to bounce the matchbox **off the ceiling** to double the possible penalty – although failure to hit the ceiling results in an immediate two-finger/sip fine. Lastly, should any **matches fall out** of the box during a sub-table manoeuvre, the current box-flicker will be forced to drain the contents of his drink in **one go.**

Bolloxed factor...

TIMBER!

 **IT'S THE OLD PUB-FAVOURITE JENGA – BUT ON THE CHEAP.**

ESSENTIAL SUPPLIES
An empty bottle. A full matchbox. Beer.

 ike building a stack of playing cards, **Timber!** offers a similar challenge to the thrill-seeking drink junkie, but one that takes its design and inspiration from the familiar pub environment.

It is simply this: players place an empty beer bottle in the middle of the table and then attempt to stack as many matches as they can on the neck. With full drinks in front of each player, participants take it in turn to add another match to the precariously-balanced, ever-growing pile of wood on top of the bottle. The **loser** is the one who successfully adds his/her match, but in doing so, **knocks the rest off** onto the table. When this happens, all players are duty-bound to shout **'Timber!'** and to mock the player who ended the game. If mocking is not sufficient, however, the penalty should be to down a drink in under 30 seconds. Or 20, if you're feeling a little harsh...

 Hints & Tips
A slightly sneaky thing to know is that a little moisture can help the matchsticks stick together...

Bolloxed factor...

BEER PONG

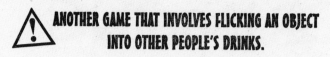

⚠️ **ANOTHER GAME THAT INVOLVES FLICKING AN OBJECT INTO OTHER PEOPLE'S DRINKS.**

ESSENTIAL SUPPLIES
Some glasses of beer. A ping-pong ball. A table.

Judging by the title and the **'essential supplies'** you're probably thinking that **Beer Pong** is just another 'flick-an-object-into-an-opponent's-beer' game. Well, you're absolutely right. Trying to get everyday objects into other people's drinks (preferably by launching them into the air) forms the backbone of many a classic drinking game and **Beer Pong** is not one to shirk hundreds of years of tradition.

Best played with either two players or two teams of two, participants should arrange the glasses of beer like a wall in front of them – four to six glasses ought to be sufficient. Then, **yes,** each player or team takes it in turn to try and get the ping-pong ball into the opposing team's glasses. Naturally, if a ball does land in a cup, then the opposing team is forced to **drink the contents.** The empty glass is then taken out of the line, leaving only the full/half-full glasses in play. Repeat until drunk. The first team or player to land a ping-pong ball in all of the opposing team's glasses, is the winner.

Hints & Tips
Ping-pong balls are very light. The occasional judicious sneeze or sneaky blow might be enough to knock it off course...

Bolloxed factor...
🍺🍺🍺🍺🍺🍺🍺

THE POOL DRINKING GAME

⚠ **AN ENTICING MIX OF TWO GREAT PUB TRADITIONS – BEER AND POOL.**

ESSENTIAL SUPPLIES
A pool table. Cues. Balls. Beer.

lay a game of pool as normal, but add these simple penalties and forfeits to spice up the green baize action. **(1)** For every shot that doesn't pot a ball – excluding foul balls – drink **one finger/sip** from your pint. **(2)** Foul shots – missing your ball, hitting an opponent's ball, moving a ball with your hand, etc. – drink **two fingers/sips. (3)** Potting the white ball, drink **four fingers/sips. (4)** Potting the black ball – when you're not supposed to – drink a hefty **eight fingers/sips.** Theoretically, the more you drink, the worse you play. And the worse you play, the more you are **forced to drink.** A vicious circle...

Variants:

Killer: Rack up the pool balls as normal. But this time, players MUST pot a ball (of any colour, except the white) whenever they visit the table. Each player gets one shot (except the player who breaks off, he/she is allowed two shots to pot a ball).

If a player pots a ball, he/she then leaves the table and lets the next player on. If a player fails to pot a ball during a visit to the table, he/she

116

Hints & Tips

Try and avoid playing this with anyone who introduces himself as "Alexsh Higginsh", you're probably gonna get beat.

loses one of three lives and incurs a two-finger/sip fine. The player with the most lives left at the end of the game, wins.

Drink The Difference: Play a game of pool as normal. But for every ball that is left on the table after the winning player has potted the black, the loser must drink a two-finger/sip penalty.

Bolloxed factor...

CHEERS!

MOUTH-LIFT TRUCK

⚠ A GAME THAT REQUIRES A STRONG SET OF TEETH OR
ASTONISHING ORAL SUCTION.

ESSENTIAL SUPPLIES
An empty bottle. Beer.

silly, throwaway game, designed to embarrass anyone who's perky enough to say **'yeah, ok. I'll do it.'** Simply place an empty bottle on the floor and challenge the players to pick it up with their mouth. Of course, it's a bit more difficult than just getting down on all fours, leaning over and picking the bottle up between your teeth. To make things difficult, players must first **stand on one leg,** holding their other leg behind their body with their right hand. Not only that, but to keep the left hand busy, it must continually keep hold of your head's right ear throughout the bottle-grabbing manoeuvre. Lift the bottle off the floor to avoid drinking a **two-finger/sip** fine. But even if you fail, it's worth it just to see how many people fall flat on their faces, or how human balance is disrupted by the presence of eight pints of lager...

Hints & Tips
Try and go first. Once that beer bottle's had everybody's lips around it, it's going to be well slippy...

Bolloxed factor...

🍾🍾🍾🍾🍾🍾🍾

BEER ROULETTE

⚠ **AN ALLURING MIX OF RUSSIAN ROULETTE AND SHOTGUN CAN-DRINKING.**

ESSENTIAL SUPPLIES
A six-pack of beer.

The frightening allure of **Russian Roulette** (one revolver, six chambers, one bullet...) is the sheer random danger, the fine line between life and death that's walked whenever the trigger is pulled.

Beer Roulette attempts to offer a similar thrill, but without the guns and the bullets. In short, one person takes an ordinary six- pack of beer/lager out of the room and shakes one of the cans. Not just a little shake. But a big, vigorous, very violent shake. Then the can is mixed up with the five unshaken cans and returned to the room, where all six are placed in a bag. One by one, the budding **Beer Roulette** players pick cans out of the bag and open them right under their noses. If yours is the beer that explodes, then you are considered **'dead',** and must sit out the next round. The survivors then knock back their opened beers and the process begins anew. The last player **'alive'** wins the game.

Hints & Tips
It helps to make sure that the cans aren't very cold either, take them out of the fridge 15 minutes before needed.

Bolloxed factor...
🍾🍾🍾🍾🍾🍾🍾🍾

BOTTLE TOPS

 MORE INDISCRIMINATE FLICKING. BUT THIS TIME, IT'S BOTTLE TOPS.

ESSENTIAL SUPPLIES
Bottled beer. Some extra bottle tops

You know the drill by now... gather a group of friends and sit everybody down in a nice, friendly, and most importantly, big circle. Each player puts an open bottled beer in front of them, with the bottle top balanced neatly (upside down) on the top of the neck. Taking it in turns, the players then use extra bottle tops to try and knock the tops off of the bottles. Throw them, spin them, flick them... whatever way you launch the tops, if you knock the top off another player's beer, they must take a drink from it. Knock it off twice and not only does the player have to drink again, but you can make up a rule and a booze-tinted consequence if the rule is broken. Knock a player's bottle top off three times and the targeted player must finish his bottle in one go.

You can keep firing bottle tops at people's beer until you miss, whereupon your turn ends and the player to your left gets a go. At no time during the game can you adjust your bottle top if it is starting to slip. Illegal bottle top intervention is punishable by a five sip fine.

 Hints & Tips
It can be a good idea to use more than just one bottle of beer each, particularly later on, when no-one can aim straight.

Bolloxed factor...

JUGS

 SORRY, LADS. THIS GAME HAS ABSOLUTELY NOTHING TO DO WITH BREASTS.

ESSENTIAL SUPPLIES
A large jug or bowl. A small glass (a half-pint one will do). Beer.

This game, say its fans, is "reminiscent of the game **Spill the Beans** but with an alcoholic twist." Fill the large jug or bowl about three-quarters full of beer and then place the glass, also three-quarters full of beer, inside the jug. With any luck, the glass should now be floating inside the jug – if it sinks, it's too full, if it capsizes there's not enough beer to weight it down sufficiently.

The **aim of the game** is simply this: each player in turn tries to **add some beer** to the floating glass **without sinking it.** The unfortunate player who finally makes the glass sink, must scoop out the glass, fill it with beer and drink the contents. Similarly, anybody jogging, nudging or bumping the table, which causes the glass to sink, gets penalised with the a pint-of-beer fine.

Hints & Tips
You're going to need quite a lot of beer to play this, so make sure you're well stocked up before the game starts.

Bolloxed factor...

BLIND IGNORANCE

> ⚠ **YOU ARE GODZILLA. I AM JAPAN. OR BONAPARTE. OR MAYBE JOHN CLEESE...**

ESSENTIAL SUPPLIES
Rizzla papers or Post-It Notes. Beer.

A guessing game with a suitably adult (i.e. Beer) twist, in many ways **Blind Ignorance** is like watching a mini-version of **What's My Line?** Using Rizzla papers or Post-It Notes, each player writes down the name of a person (real or fictional). Then, turning to the person on their right, and WITHOUT showing that person the name of the character/personality, stick the bit of paper onto their forehead.

The identity of everyone in the group is now plainly obvious, apart that is from your own as you can't see what has been written down and slapped onto your skull. Players have to take it in turns to ask key questions about the person that they are supposed to be, to which the other players can only answer **'yes'** or **'no'**. Guessing players can continue to ask questions (i.e. Am I a man? Am I a famous actor? etc.) until they receive **'no'** as an answer.

When this happens, their go then ends, and play passes to the next player who attempts to guess his/her secret identity. Players who have successfully deciphered the clues and discovered the name of the personage scribbled on their forehead, can remove the name-revealing sticker from their heads. And the last person to work it out...?

Hints & Tips

Try and be imaginative when choosing a character. A good, sneaky one is to choose the person themselves. That's always hard to guess.

Rearrange **'finger'**, **'fine'** and **'five'** into a sentence to get your answer. If you want to make the game a little more 'exciting', you can make each player suffer a suitable penalty each time they ask a question and get 'no' as a reply. A couple of sips should be about right.

Bolloxed factor...

CHEERS!

DANGEROUS DARTS

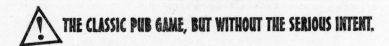 **THE CLASSIC PUB GAME, BUT WITHOUT THE SERIOUS INTENT.**

ESSENTIAL SUPPLIES
A pub dart board. Darts. Beer.

 angerous Darts, or **Beer Darts** as it's often known, is a quick-and-easy game that favours both those with skill and dexterity, and those who just hurl the darts at the board hoping for the best.

Blending traditional play with the simplicity of Jim Bowen's **Bullseye,** play evolves as follows: each player steps up to throw his/her three arrows at the board. Scoring can continue as usual (or you can just forget all about it, the choice is yours), because it's not how much you score with your darts, it's where the darts land on the board that determines the penalties that the players incur. For example:

(1) If your dart lands in a **black** area, drink **two-fingers/sips** of beer.

(2) If your dart lands in a **white** area, breathe a sigh of relief and **do nothing.**

(3) If your dart **misses** the board completely and thwunks loudly into the wall, drink **four fingers/sips** – add an extra one if the dart falls to the floor and sticks in it.

Hints & Tips
You'll probably be tempted to aim for a lot of '7's, but make sure you look out for that dastardly '13' – it's not very far away.

(4) If your dart lands in the number **13**, drink **five fingers/sips.**

(5) If your dart hits a **'double',** your **opponent** must drink **three fingers/sips** from their pint.

(6) If your dart hits a **'triple',** your **opponent** must drink **four fingers/sips** from their pint.

(7) If your dart hits the **'Bullseye',** your opponent must drink **four fingers/sips** from their pint.

(8) If your dart lands in the number **7**, your opponent must drink **seven fingers/sips** from their pint.

Bolloxed factor...

ICE CUBE RAFT RACE

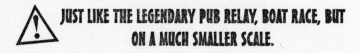

⚠ JUST LIKE THE LEGENDARY PUB RELAY, BOAT RACE, BUT ON A MUCH SMALLER SCALE.

ESSENTIAL SUPPLIES
An ice cube tray. Shots of your favourite spirit. Some straws.

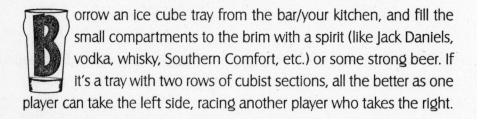

Borrow an ice cube tray from the bar/your kitchen, and fill the small compartments to the brim with a spirit (like Jack Daniels, vodka, whisky, Southern Comfort, etc.) or some strong beer. If it's a tray with two rows of cubist sections, all the better as one player can take the left side, racing another player who takes the right.

The idea is simply to drink each compartment dry through a straw, before moving onto the next one, and then the next one, until all of the ice cube tray compartments have been emptied. Whoever finishes first wins the **Ice Cube Raft Race** and condemns the loser to a forfeit of their choice. Having to provide the spirits for the next race is usually a fairly effective one.

Variants:
Ice Cube Relay Race. Try using two, or even three, ice cube trays and two teams of players. To change the game into a relay, put the trays on different tables and make the competing players run to the next table after they have drained the liquids out of their own tray. They then pass

Hints & Tips

Putting a different spirit in every cube can add a certain frisson to this already fairly lethal game – just work along the bar's optics.

the straw onto the next player, who starts to drink each compartment dry in his own tray. As an amusing addition, a line of peanuts that can only be eaten one-by-one with the player only allowed to use his/her mouth can be used to break things up.

Bolloxed factor...

CHEERS!

POWER HOUR

⚠️ **POWER HOUR? SOUNDS SUSPICIOUSLY LIKE A 'STUPID HOUR'...**

ESSENTIAL SUPPLIES
Lots of beer. Tremendous stamina and bladder control.

Although it's not really a game, the **Power Hour** is an endurance challenge, a game with no penalties, shouting, gesture-making, coin-spinning, card-holding or die-flipping. It's a test of a beer-drinker's manhood, an event, like the **London Marathon**, which should only be attempted once, just so you can say that you've done it. Here's how it works: quite simply, the **Power Hour** challenges you to swig a gulp of beer, every minute, for an entire hour. That's it. Sound easy? Can you make it through the time-limit without missing a gulp or going to the bathroom? Any break with the single **Power Hour** rule, and players will be penalised a whole pint of beer which must be consumed within 30 seconds, so as not to further disrupt the vital gulp-per-minute schedule.

Variants:
The Century Club: Uses the same basic idea as the **Power Hour**, but wannabe **Century Club** members swig a gulp of beer every minute for 100 minutes. Bloody fools.

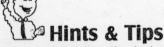

Hints & Tips
Make sure you've got plenty of beer lined up, you don't want to waste time by having to go to the bar, do you?

Bolloxed factor...

BEER SQUARE

⚠ **THE INNOCENT NOUGHTS & CROSSES BECOMES FULL PINTS AND HALF-PINTS.**

ESSENTIAL SUPPLIES
Nine beer mats. Nine pints of beer. Two players.

A beer-tinged version of the old **Tic-Tac-Toe** game (**Noughts & Crosses** to the rest of you), the rules for **Beer Square** are wonderfully concise and simple. Arrange your nine beer mats in a 3x3 square and decide which of the two players will go first. After this, each player takes it in turn to either put a pint of beer on the table or to drink from a pint of beer that's already on the table. The aim of the game is to get three of a kind in a horizontal, vertical or diagonal row – i.e. three full pints, three half-full pints, or three empty glasses. Each turn, players can **(a)** drink half of a full pint leaving a half-full glass on the table. **(b)** drink from a half-full pint, leaving an empty glass on the table. **(c)** add a pint glass to the 3 x 3 square, either leaving it full or drinking from it to create a half-full glass or an empty glass. Glasses must be replaced on the mat they were removed from by the players. The **winner** is the person who organises the board so that there are three glasses of the same type in a row. The loser doesn't pay a drinking forfeit (he/she will have consumed a fair amount of beer during the game). But he/she does have to stump up for the next round. That's **nine beers please barman...** ouch.

Hints & Tips
The player who forms a line of full pint glasses is the one who gets least drunk, and thus has the best chance to win.

Bolloxed factor...

🍾🍾🍾🍾🍾🍾🍾🍾🍾

THUMPER

⚠ **ABOUT AS FAR AWAY FROM BAMBI'S LOVABLE BUNNY PAL AS YOU'RE LIKELY TO GET.**

ESSENTIAL SUPPLIES
Lots of beer. A table. A good sense of rhythm.

lthough there is some word-play in **Thumper,** the bulk of this fast-paced drinking game revolves around making silly gestures with hands, feet, torso, if you can move it, use it... To play, gather a group of open-minded people around a table.

To distinguish themselves from one-another, each person must invent a gesture to represent him/her. When the gestures have been revealed (players should do this **twice** in an attempt to imprint the strange movements on the brains of the other players), everybody at the table should then start drumming on the surface with their fingers.

One player says: **"What is the name of the game?"** To which everyone should reply in unison: **"Thumper!"** The first player now says: **"Why do we play it?"** To which everyone should gleefully yell: **"To get pissed"**.

Now comes the tricky part... the first player then makes **his gesture,** followed by **the gesture of one of the other players.** The player to whom the second gesture belongs, must quickly respond to this by flourishing their gesture, followed by another players.

All the while everybody is drumming... Anybody who stops drumming, must drink **a** suitable fine. Anybody who performs the wrong gesture,

130

Hints & Tips

Try and make your gesture fairly complicated, that way it won't be remembered so often — unless you like having to drink a lot.

or gestures out of turn is also penalised. Players cannot make the gesture of the player immediately previous to their go. If they do, they face a double fine.

Bolloxed factor...

131

TURBO CUPS

⚠ **PASS THE PLASTIC CUP OF BEER IN THIS PUB-FRIENDLY RELAY RACE.**

ESSENTIAL SUPPLIES
One cup per player. A table. Beer.

E ssentially, little more than a twisted relay race with beer, **Turbo Cups** takes the traditional **Boat Race** idea, swaps plastic cups for pint glasses and adds a touch more skill to the proceedings. The game requires two teams, ideally with about three or four players in each one.

Form two teams of three or four, and line up the teams on opposite sides of a handily-placed table. Fill one cup per person with beer and arrange them in a neat row so that the players can get at them easily. When all this is ready, the first two members of each time must approach the table and start the **Turbo Cups** race. After somebody either shouts **'go!'**, slaps a hand down on the table, drops a handkerchief on the floor (whatever), these two players must **drink their cup of beer** as quickly as they can. Once finished, they must next speedily place the empty cup on the lip of the table, so that one half of the cup's base overhangs the edge. Finally, they must then, using their forefinger, **flip the cup up** onto the table, trying to make it land upside down. If the player succeeds in doing this, their go is over and the second player in the team can approach the table, drink his/her beer and attempt to flip over the next cup. Players must stay at the table, continually flipping the overhanging cup, for as long as it takes for it to land upside down. The first team to **(a)** drink all their beer and **(b)** to flip all their cups correctly, wins the race.

Hints & Tips

It's a good idea to appoint a referee, someone to make sure that all the beer is actually drained before the flipping starts, for example.

Variants:

To make the game last longer, simply introduce a second round to the proceedings. This time, prepare **three cups** of beer per person. The first round takes place as normal (drink beer, flip cup, next player, etc.), while the second round **doubles** the stakes – team members must drink down two cups of beer and flip both cups upside down before they are allowed to leave the table. Again, the first team to successfully complete rounds one and two is the winner.

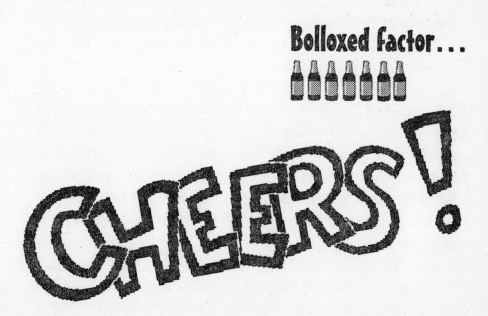

Bolloxed factor...

CHEERS!

BEAT THE BARMAN

⚠️ **AN OUTRAGEOUS GAME THAT WE SUSPECT VERY FEW OF YOU WILL ACTUALLY PLAY.**

ESSENTIAL SUPPLIES
A friendly barman. Arrogance. No fear. A £10 note.

A silly game, best played at the end of the night (when you should be high on Dutch Courage and therefore have the **balls of an elephant**), and in a pub where you and the barstaff are extremely good friends. If you don't, you face getting shouted at, beaten up, thrown out, arrested and, worst of all, barred. Because as far as the urban myth is concerned, nobody wins a game of **Beat The Barman.** Then again, nobody really loses or draws either. So, for all you buzz-craving, insane drinkers, here's how the game (such as it is) works:

(1) The player walks up to the bar and orders a short (i.e. a shot of whiskey, vodka, gin, etc.) with no ice and no poncey lemon slices. **(2)** The crafty player then pays for said short with far too much money (say, a tenner) **(3)** While the barman nips back to the cash register to get the change, the player quickly downs the short, hides the glass and puts on a confused, yet innocent, smile. **(4)** When the barman returns with the change, go back to step **(1).**

Short on luck and skill, but big on confrontation, a game of **Beat The Barman** can end in several ways. Firstly, if the player falls over in a

Hints & Tips
You should only contemplate getting involved in this game if you're astride a jet-powered motorbike on a highway to oblivion. Clearly.

sorry, drunken heap then the pub wins. If the barman visits any violence upon the player's person as a result of his/her cheekiness, then the game is considered drawn. Similarly, the game is also deemed drawn if the management eject the arrogant player from the pub and bar him for life. Finally, if the pub is closed as a result of the player's actions (not if last orders have been shouted and it's the accepted chucking-out time), then the drinker wins the day.

Bolloxed factor...

BEER BUNGEE

⚠️ **DANGEROUS SPORTS MEETS ALCOHOL IN THE SAFEST ENVIRONMENT AVAILABLE – THE BEER GARDEN.**

ESSENTIAL SUPPLIES
A bungee cord. Beer.

Opportunities to play **Beer Bungee** don't tend to pop up very often down your local boozer. Fruit machines? Certainly. A game of darts or pool? Most pubs have one. But a 20ft bungee cord? It's not exactly something that most barman keep behind the crisps. That said, in most pubs, you'd be hard-pressed to find a clear 20ft to play the game in. But no matter, with a few alterations, **Beer Bungee** is still a perfectly playable drinking game. Albeit a downright stupid one. In ideal circumstances, you should attach one end of the 20ft bungee to a pub door or wall, making sure there's a gap of about 30ft between the wall/door and the bar. But as this isn't always possible, **Beer Bungee** is best played outside in a large garden. Fix or tie the end of the bungee cord to a solid, heavy object (a tree, a truck, etc.) and place the glasses of beer on a table about 30ft away. Then all you have to do is attach an eager player to the other end of the bungee and watch as they try to reach the beer on the table. If you measure it correctly, the players should just about be able to reach the beer on the table. But as they are at full-stretch, it's almost impossible to get the beer back without spilling it all over them. A silly game to play, but a fun one to watch.

Hints & Tips
The truly devious will place each drink slightly further away than the preceeding one, with hilarious consequences.

Bolloxed Factor...
🍾🍾🍾🍾🍾🍾🍾🍾🍾

SIXTY SECONDS

⚠ **WHEN CLOCK-WATCHING CAN BE FUN. NEXT TIME:**
WE LINK DRINKING AND WATCHING PAINT DRY...

ESSENTIAL SUPPLIES
A watch or clock with a second hand/digital display. Beer.

uick and easy – this is almost a fast-track to alcoholic oblivion. **Sixty Seconds** is another game that bases its drinking around random numbers. In this case, instead of a cards, dice, money or characters in movies, all you need to play is an analogue clock (one with a second hand) or a good digital timepiece with a second-by-second count. To play, each player picks a selection of ten numbers between 1 and 60 (i.e. 1-10, 11-20, 31-40, and so on) and whenever the second hand/digital count reaches a player's set of numbers, that player has to keep drinking until the count passes by the last number in their sequence. And that's it. A good game if you're stuck in the middle of a watch factory, with no cards, dice, money, TV and have a large supply of beer to get through

Hints & Tips
It's probably best to hang the watch up somewhere so that there's no chance of it becoming beer-sodden and stopping.

Bolloxed factor...

SHOTGUN

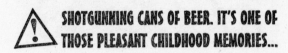

⚠ **SHOTGUNNING CANS OF BEER. IT'S ONE OF THOSE PLEASANT CHILDHOOD MEMORIES...**

ESSENTIAL SUPPLIES
Cans of beer. A pointy implement (a compass point, sharp knife).

Another traditional party pastime, Shotgunning isn't really a drinking game in itself, but it can be adapted to fit in with many of the games mentioned in this book. Especially if used as a drinking penalty. For those of you who aren't familiar with the concept of shotgunning, here's a quick recap.

Grab a can of beer. But before you open it, **puncture a small hole** near the bottom of the can with a knife, a fork prong or something suitable pointy and sharp. Then simply **place your mouth over the hole** (watch out for any sharp edges when you do this), raise your head up so the can is being held vertically and then open the can.

The pressurised beer will then be forced through the new hole at a tremendous rate, and the drinker must attempt to swallow it quickly without spilling any over their clothes, presuming they want to stay dry. The faster you drink, the more drunk you'll become (we find this is a rule that holds true for almost any kind of drinking endeavour). So surely this must be perfect as a fine for persistently bad games-players.

Variants:
Shotgun Boat Race Organise two teams into traditional **Boat Race** setups (i.e. a line of four players, beer... you should remember the score from **Turbo Cups** on page 132). But instead of drinking pints one at a time and putting the empty glasses on your head, each player must

Hints & Tips

You probably shouldn't try this with any of those extra-large party cans that some offies sell, but if you do – we salute you!

shotgun a can, then crush it on their forehead before the next player can start drinking... Funnily enough, the crushing bit tends to get easier as the evening wears on, but be careful or you'll look very strange the next day.

Bolloxed factor...

VIKING

⚠ **ALL THE ELEMENTS OF A TRADITIONAL WORD GAME, BUT WITHOUT THE WORDS.**

ESSENTIAL SUPPLIES
Beer. A knowledge of ancient Nordic headgear.

nother simple game whose characteristics set it apart from the card, dice, cash and TV-based games that make up the most popular drink-a-thons. It is, however, quite similar in style to the way that word games function, with the obvious difference that nobody in a game of **Viking** is allowed to speak.

Here's how it works: The players (up to ten can play) sit in a circle and one person is chosen to start the game. This player quickly makes **"Viking horns,"** created by sticking their thumbs in their ears and wiggling/waving the remaining fingers. Then the player stops, claps his hands together once, and points at another person in the circle. This next player is also required to make the embarrassing sign of the viking; the difference this time, however, is that the players either side of the new viking also come into play and must **'steer the boat'**. What this means is that the two flanking players must make a rowing action – the person on the left of the viking rows to the left, the person on the right rows to the right. If all this happens quickly and correctly, the viking can then stop wiggling his hands in his/her ears, clap hands and pass the viking buck to another player in the circle.

Play then repeats until either a viking misses their cue, or one of the flanking rowers forgets to make the appropriate oaring action. Whoever misses their action, must drink a penalty.

Hints & Tips

It's sensible to play this in a pub where you're well known. Your reputation will be amusingly enhanced for months afterwards.

Variants:

Bunnies: Instead of viking horns, how about floppy bunny ears? As if you wouldn't have been able to guess the action, the player puts two hands to his head and wiggles them like rabbit ears. When this happens, the player on the left must raise and waggle their right hand only, while the person on the right must waggle the left hand as an ear. Like **Viking,** the bunny-elect then claps and point at another player transfer the bunny curse onwards.

Bolloxed factor...

MASTER OF THE THUMB

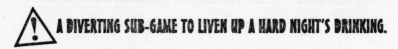

⚠ A DIVERTING SUB-GAME TO LIVEN UP A HARD NIGHT'S DRINKING.

ESSENTIAL SUPPLIES
Beer.

This game can be played in conjunction with any other game featured in this book or as an extra rule during the course of an evening's gaming. The game starts by nominating a player to be the eponymous **Master Of The Thumb.**

While it offers no advantages in the game that it's added to, the designated **Master Of The Thumb** can certainly spice the night up by using the one special power that he/she possesses. In short, the digit-king can, at any time, place his/her thumb down on the edge of the table. If it is left there, anybody who notices that the thumb-master has placed a strategic thumb down, can emulate the move by placing their own thumb on the table.

The last person to notice the thumb movement loses this **Master Of The Thumb** sub-game and is forced to drink a suitable penalty. The loser then becomes the new **Master Of The Thumb** and whatever game the group was originally playing, continues.

Variants:
Master Of The Nose: (the nasal chief can kick the process off by placing their forefinger on the end of their nose); **Arms Crossed** (the

Hints & Tips
When you're the master, try and use some other action to disguise what you're doing. Like standing up, raising yourself by the thumbs...

designated arm-crosser keeps their arms, er, crossed. The last one to notice and emulate, drinks); **Hands-On-Head** (fairly obvious, don't you think); and so on.

Bolloxed factor...

CHEERS!

CHAPTER 5

TONGUE-TWISTERS & WORD GAMES

Highly portable (all you need is your mouth, your brain and a couple of useful limbs), drinking games based on word association, spelling and name-calling, are amongst the most popular boozy entertainment you can find. And here you'll find the best of the bunch. It's the definitive collection of the old (**Fuzzy Duck, Ibble Dibble**) and the new (**Drink Don't Think, Sentences**), all games designed to briefly challenge the mind and, the longer you play them, to lead you by the todger into the welcoming arms of alcohol-powered disfunction. They can be played anywhere too – in the pub, at home, at the airport while you're waiting for a plane, because most of them don't require any props. So pick a game (we recommend **Drink Don't Think** or the anarchic **Fizz Buzz**) and try your luck. See how long it takes for your mouth to stop working and your hands to refuse to communicate with your head.

I NEVER DID

 **A GAME THAT REQUIRES A KEEN MIND AND A LOW EMBARRASSMENT THRESHOLD.**

ESSENTIAL SUPPLIES
Beer. Spirits.

 simple, alcoholic version of the party-favourite **Truth Or Dare** – a game that will undoubtedly start off slow and cautious, but that just as inevitably gets better the longer you play and the more you drink...

Gather a group of friends around a table, or in a circle on the floor. Select one player to begin. This player kicks off the game by saying **"I never did..."** followed by something that the player actually has done. Everybody around the table who also has done the exploit mentioned by the speaking player then drinks an appropriate drinking fine. Then the next player announces that he/she **'never did'** something and play continues around the circle. As the inhibitions start to crumble due to excessive alcohol consumption later in the game, the deeds mentioned will alter from the largely innocent ("I never did go to the supermarket"), to the risky ("I never did lie and say I was busy") to the downright confrontational, ("I never did sleep with Dave's wife").

 Hints & Tips
Don't ever play this game with anyone you've really done something terrible, and secret, too. It'll come out...

Bolloxed factor...

BULLSH*T

⚠ A GAME OF WITS, FINESSE AND LOUD, UNCOUTH
SHOUTING IN PUBLIC PLACES.

ESSENTIAL SUPPLIES
Beer. Spirits.

As usual, for this fast-paced, slightly bawdy word game, gather a group of friends together in a circle or around a table, and select one of the players to go first. This player kicks off the game by announcing: "one day I was walking down the street when I saw [name of player two] taking a shit!". Player two then counters loudly with: **"bullshit!"**. Quickly player one chips in with: **"who shit?"** to which player two adds **"[name of player three] shit"**. Now it's player three's turn to say **"bullshit!".** Player two then says **"who shit?"** to which player three can then say **"[name of player four] shit"**. Once the game has completed a circle of the players involved, the players can nominate any player in the circle in any order. Penalties are awarded for hesitation, for speaking out of turn or for slurring your words. To make things more difficult, try the game by assigning different names to the players, i.e. Player one, player two, etc; or celebrity names; animal names; and so on. The only other rules are that if two people duel verbally with each other for more than three times then they both have to drink. And if a player mucks up his/her go more than three times, they are condemned to finish the rest of their beer/short.

Hints & Tips
This is another game to be careful about who's overhearing you. Potential girl-friends are not going to be impressed.

Bolloxed Factor...
🍾🍾🍾🍾🍾🍾🍾🍾

ACTOR & MOVIE

 A SIMPLE GAME OF MOVIE KNOWLEDGE ENLIVENED BY A SMATTERING OF LOVELY BOOZE

ESSENTIAL SUPPLIES
Beer. Spirits. A loose tongue.

Another simple knowledge game, where 'you either know it or you don't' and if 'you don't' you'll get into alcoholic trouble quicker than everybody else. This game's theme is the movies and although the rules of play are simple, an extensive knowledge of films, actors and actresses is a distinct advantage.

Here's how it works: gather a group of players and select somebody to go first. This player then names an **actor or** an **actress** and the rest of the players, in turn around the group, attempt to **name a film** that the named actor/actress has been in (30 seconds are allowed for deep thought). I.e. if player one says **'Bill Pullman'**, player two could mention **'Independence Day'**, player three might say **'Lost Highway'** and so on. The first person who can't guess movie that the relevant star has appeared in, or says a movie that the star did NOT appear in, has to drink a penalty.

And there's a neat twist – when somebody can't think of a movie the actor/actress has appeared in, the other players get 60 seconds to try and think of some extra ones. The total of these films is counted up after the minute has passed and the player paying the penalty must

Hints & Tips
Watch lots of Wim Wenders films and buy the Time Out movie guide if you want to be any good at this diabolically difficult game.

then **drink for X seconds** (where X is the number of films that the other players managed to think of).

Unsurprisingly, a keen knowledge of little-known Euro-actors and arthouse is a distinct advantage. Everybody can name some movies that **Bruce Willis** has been in. But how many people will be able to list the filmography of **Koji Yakusyo?**

Bolloxed factor...

CHEERS!

BUZZ

⚠ **A FUN AND SIMPLE DRINKING GAME THAT TESTS THOSE LONG FORGOTTEN MATHS SKILLS.**

ESSENTIAL SUPPLIES
Beer. Spirits.

This well-known game may sound easy to play, but its simplicity is merely a smokescreen for a devilish word game that's actually much trickier than it first appears. Start the game, by sitting everyone down in a circle and by picking one player to start. This player then begins to count, saying the number **"1"**. The person to their immediate left then says **"2"**, the next player says **"3"**, and so on around the group.

Things start to get interesting, however, when the count gets to either 7, 11, a multiple of 7 or 11, or a number that features 7 in its digits. As soon as this happens, the player must say **'Buzz'** instead of the number, i.e. 1, 2, 3, 4, 5, 6, Buzz, 8, 9, 10, Buzz, 12, 13, Buzz, 15, etc.)

Also, as soon as someone says **Buzz** you switch directions – so if the game was rolling to the left, it now stops, reverses and moves around to the right. Again, if anybody hesitates, says a 7, 11, multiple of 7 or 11, or a number with 7 in it, or says **Buzz** when they don't have to, the usual drinking penalty (for example, two fingers/sips per mistake) applies. Easy to learn, difficult to master, repeat the game, getting faster and faster, until the participants can no longer stand, let alone count from 1-10.

Hints & Tips

We can't help you here. All we suggest is that you try and work a little bit ahead so that you have some idea what's coming. It won't last long.

Variants: Fizz Buzz

This version plays in the same way as **Buzz** above, only that instead of numbers containing or divisible by 7 and 11, the game challenges players by changing the magic number to 3. That means that no number that's a multiple of 3 or features a 3 can be said. Instead the player must substitute the numeral with either **'Buzz'** or **'Fizz'** – i.e. 1, 2, Fizz, 4, 5, Buzz, 7, 8, Buzz, etc. Simply put, if a player says **'Buzz'** the direction of play reverses, but if the player says **'Fizz'** the play continues in the same direction. Any mistake is penalised by a drink. Believe it, this can get incredibly confusing.

Bizz Buzz Bang

Now it gets really tricky. **Bizz Buzz Bang** takes the obvious step and introduces different words for different numbers and their multiples. In this case, **Bizz** equals 3, **Buzz** represents 5 and **Bang** takes the place of 7. So whenever a 3 or a multiple of 3 comes up during the count you say **'Bizz'** (3, 6, 9, 12, 13, 15, etc.); whenever a 5 or multiple of 5 comes up you say **'Buzz'** (5, 10, 15, 20, etc.); and when a 7 or multiple of 7 comes up you say **'Bang'** (7, 14, 17, 21, 27, 28).

Finally, if you have a number that has more than two properties, you say both words – i.e. 15 is divisible by 3 (continued overleaf)

and 5 so you would say **'Bizz- Buzz'**; 35 contains a 3, and is divisible by 5 and 7, so this warrants a **'Bizz-Buzz-Bang'**. Thus, a game would unfold like this: 1, 2, Bizz, 4, Buzz, Bizz, Bang, 8, Bizz, Buzz, 11, Bizz, Bizz, Bang, Bizz- Buzz, 16, and so on. As usual, anybody who makes a mistake, drinks. If anyone can work out that they have.

Bolloxed factor…

CATEGORIES

⚠️ THINK. DRINK. THINK. DRINK. REPEAT UNTIL 'SOBER' SOUNDS LIKE 'SOFA'.

ESSENTIAL SUPPLIES
Beer. Spirits.

nother relatively simple game, worth learning because it can be used as part of the **Multi** card-based drinking game. Gather people together in a rough circle and select an eager player to go first. He/she must think of an appropriate category, i.e. Division 1 football teams, and then each subsequent player must name an item/thing that fits into the category – so player two could say **Birmingham City**, player three might mumble **Ipswich** and so on. Hesitation is punishable with a drinking penalty, as is the player who can't think of a new item/thing to add to the category. This player then drinks the penalty and chooses a new category. Then the game begins anew. Told you it was simple.

Variants: A Ship Came Into the Harbour

The same game, but with a salty, nautical spin. The first player announces that: "a ship came into the harbour carrying... **a cargo of** beer", then the players around the table must name different brands of beer or lager (Heineken, Kronenbourg, Carlsberg, etc.) Whoever can't think of a new kind of beer, then **pays the penalty** and picks a new category. I.e. "a ship came into the harbour carrying... a cargo of cigarettes." (Marlboro, Camel, Silk Cut, etc.)

Hints & Tips
Try and choose relatively easy categories, because the game is more fun played like that. 'Mongolian Cheeses' is not clever.

Bolloxed factor...
🍾🍾🍾🍾🍾🍾

153

DRINK DON'T THINK

⚠ **BY FAR THIS AUTHOR'S FAVOURITE DRINKING GAME. FUN, DEMANDING AND DEADLY...**

ESSENTIAL SUPPLIES
Beer. Spirits.

ypically simple yet addictively playable, **Drink Don't Think** is one of the easiest/trickiest drinking games ever devised. And that's just the start of the seriously twisted thinking that this game is going to inspire in you.

Here's how it works: gather your group of friends and select a player to go first. This player then kicks off the game by saying the name of a famous person, either a **celebrity** (Johnny Depp, Bruce Forsythe) or a well-known **cartoon character** (Donald Duck, Mickey Mouse).

The next player to go can then say the name of another celebrity, a name that must begin with the first letter of the previous celeb's surname. I.e. player one might start with **Emma Thompson**, so player two would have to say a name beginning with **'T'**, **Terence Stamp**. Player three therefore has to think of a name that begins with an **'S'**, **Steve McManaman**, and so on.

The extra rules are simple: while a player thinks of a name he/she has to continually sip from their drink; if a player says a name that has a surname and a forename that begin with the same letter, i.e. **Charlie**

Hints & Tips

Panic is the enemy in this game, above all else just try and stay completely, utterly calm. Otherwise you're going to lose it big-time.

Chaplin, the direction of play is reversed. Names cannot be reused or repeated, if this happens the offending player must down the rest of their drink. Finally, players that cannot think of a name, must drink a two-finger/sip penalty. Continue forever.

Bolloxed factor...

155

FUZZY DUCK

 Fuzzy Duck? Reverse the D and the F and giggle at the rudeness of it all...

ESSENTIAL SUPPLIES
Beer. Spirits.

Herd your favoured friends into a circle and spin a coin to decide who goes first (preferably somebody who knows how to play the game). Player one starts the game by saying: **"Fuzzy Duck"**. The person to the left, player two, follows this opening gambit by either announcing: **"Fuzzy Duck"** or **"Does he?"** If the player plumps for saying **"Fuzzy Duck"**, the game continues and moves onto player three, who also has the opportunity to say **"Fuzzy Duck"** or **"Does he?"** If, however, a player decides to say **"Does he?"** play is reversed (moving anticlockwise) and instead of **"Fuzzy Duck"**, players have to say **"Ducky Fuzz."** If player says **"Does he?"** again, the direction changes back and **"Ducky Fuzz"** returns to the original **"Fuzzy Duck".**

Players drink a penalty if they say **"Fuzzy Duck"** when they should say **"Ducky Fuzz"** (and vice versa) or if they speak out of turn. Or indeed if they accidentally say something rude.

Hints & Tips
Somebody may latch on to the idea that it's clever to say 'does he' a lot. Well, it's not if everyone else does.

Bolloxed Factor...

156

LETTERS

 MINIMUM SUPPLIES. MINIMUM THOUGHT. MAXIMUM BEER INTAKE.

ESSENTIAL SUPPLIES
Beer. Spirits.

Gather a group of players into a circle and nominate somebody to start the game. The rules are short and sweet: player one calls out a letter and the rest of the people in the group take it in turns to call out words that begin with that letter – no plurals, no foreign languages, no past participles allowed. The game ends when a word is repeated or a player is unable to think of a new word. The losing player then drains the contents of his/her drink as a penalty and play begins again with a new letter.

CHEERS!

 Hints & Tips

Swallowing a dictionary won't actually help you think of more words, but it may help line your stomach.

Bolloxed factor...

ONE RED HEN

⚠ **A DRINKING GAME WITH LIVE POULTRY COULD BE A RECIPE FOR DISASTER...**

ESSENTIAL SUPPLIES
Beer. Spirits.

riends. Circle. You should know the drill by now. Most importantly, however, players must nominate a **'leader',** and it is the leader's responsibility to memorise the sentences (in order) below.

To the Judge, Queen, and country!
One red hen, and a couple of ducks.
Three brown bear.
Four running hare.
Five frolicking fillies.
Six simple Simons.
Seven salty seamen, sailing the seven seas.
Eight elongated elephants elevating elegantly in an elevator.
Nine nimble nymphomaniacs kneeling nicely in their nighties in a nunnery.
Ten, I am not a fig plucker, nor a fig plucker's son. But, I'll pluck figs till the fig plucking's done.

Here's how it all works:
Each of the lines must be repeated by the players in the circle after the leader has said them. Then they must take a drink. For example, the leader starts the game by saying **"To the Judge, Queen, and country!"** [takes a quick drink]. Everybody in the circle then takes it in turn to repeat this first sentence, taking a sip of their drinks after

Hints & Tips

Any unwitting obscenities uttered in the last line of the chant should be punished especially severely. A double penalty should suffice.

they've said it. Then the leader ups the stakes and says the second line: **"One red hen, and a couple of ducks."** The other players in the group must then repeat **the whole passage** thus far, i.e. "To the Judge, Queen, and country! One red hen, and a couple of ducks." Then the leader raises the difficulty again by saying the third line on its own: "Three Brown Bear." Again, the other players in the group must then repeat **the whole passage:** "To the judge, Queen, and country! One red hen, and a couple of ducks. Three Brown Bear." Everybody takes a **quick swig** of their drink after each passage is read out. Anyone who gets any of the sentences wrong, or in the incorrect order, must **finish** the rest of their drink (at least half-a-pint). The game continues until players have managed to say the full ten line passage correctly.

Bolloxed factor...

🍾🍾🍾🍾🍾🍾

QUESTIONS

⚠ EXACTLY HOW DRUNK DO YOU WANT TO GET, PLAYER ONE?

ESSENTIAL SUPPLIES
Beer. Spirits.

All you need is a room full of drinkers and a dirty mind to play this potentially controversial game. This is a game where the object is simply to ask other players questions that can only be answered with a **'yes'** or a **'no'**. Obviously, the more personal the questions are, the better and more interesting the game becomes. Questions like **"does your girlfriend scream while having sex?"** for example, are much more preferable to "did you go to the cinema last night?" Behind this simple process, however, lurk a couple of rules that guide the questioning and dish out the penalties.

For starters, players can only ask one question at a time, to one player at a time and the questions must be answerable by **'yes'** or **'no'**. Anybody who asks a question that is not answerable with a 'yes/no' response (i.e. "how many cats do you have?"), must drink a booze-related fine.

In addition, the player who is asked the question must **immediately** ask another question to another player. **Any hesitation** in answering the question, laughing, or doing anything else apart from asking another player a question, incurs a **punishment.** Putting a question to the player who has just asked you a question, is punishable by a drink. Questions can only be asked once and anybody who repeats a question (i.e. on the same subject) must drink the appropriate fine.

Hints & Tips
Avoid playing this game with anyone who already knows a potentially embarrassing secret about you. Like your mum, for instance.

Regular players will find that the best way to play **Questions** is to keep a couple of posers in your head in advance, a mix of the innocent ("is that a red jumper you're wearing?") and the slightly risqué ("we can see your nipples, are you cold?"). A variant of this game can be seen in the fabulous play **Rosencrantz and Guildenstern Are Dead.** The tennis court scene to be exact.

Bolloxed factor...

161

RHYME

⚠ A GAME FOR ASPIRING POETS AND LOVERS OF LANGUAGE EVERYWHERE.

ESSENTIAL SUPPLIES
Beer. Spirits.

 similar game to **Letters**, **Rhyme** is a drink-a-thon with an obvious twist. As its title suggests, once the players are sitting comfortably in their group and a player has been picked to go first, the aim of the game is to think of as many rhyming words as possible.

Player one starts off the process by saying a word (say, **"think"**). The other players, answering in turn, must then come up with words that rhyme with the first player's word (i.e. "drink", "blink", "clink", "sink", "kink", "pink", etc.). Play ends when a word is **repeated,** a non-rhyming word is offered, or when a **player cannot think** of a suitable word (i.e. "bink"). The violator then endures a drinking penalty and play begins again with a **new** word.

 Hints & Tips

In a big group, it's wise to have a few really hard-to-rhyme words up your sleeves. Like 'oranges' for example.

Bolloxed Factor...

🍾🍾🍾🍾🍾🍾

SENTENCES

 WHO SAYS THAT ENGLISH LANGUAGE STUDIES IS BORING?

ESSENTIAL SUPPLIES
Beer. Spirits.

ircle of friends in place, leading player nominated, a game of **Sentences** (a tricky word game that's much more difficult than its simplistic rules suggest) can begin. Player one kicks things off by saying a **random** word. The next player must then say a word that helps form a sentence but doesn't finish it. The next player must do the same and so on around the group.

For example in a four-player game: player one says **"Fish"**; player two says **"love"**; player three says **"swimming"**; player four says **"in"**, player one says **"the"**; player two says **"deep"**; player three says **"blue"**; player four says **"sea"** and the game ends.

Play continues around the circle until somebody either: **(a)** says a word that doesn't make sense in the context of the sentence, **(b)** hesitates too long, **(c)** is the third person to add an adjective or **(d)** accidentally finishes the sentence. When this happens, the losing player drinks a suitable boozy forfeit. Play then begins with a new word.

 Hints & Tips

'And" can become such a useful and eventually irritating word that you may want to ban it from the start.

Bolloxed Factor...

163

STATES

A FUN, CHALLENGING GAME. BUT DON'T PLAY IT WITH ANY AMERICAN HISTORY STUDENTS...

ESSENTIAL SUPPLIES
Beer. Spirits.

There are two versions of the **States** games and for us Brits, the simplest one (**Guess The States**) is probably the best. As usual, it involves a group of players and a nominated leader. The idea is simply to name each one of the 50 US states – easy for our Yankee cousins, perhaps, but slightly tricky for the rest of us. Player one simply begins by mentioning a state, i.e. **Texas**, and play continues until a player either cannot think of a new state or says a state that has already been referenced. Naturally, the loser drinks an appropriate fine, say half-a-pint of beer or a shot of spirits.

Variants: Counties

Unsurprisingly, the idea is to name each one of England's counties, a task that's actually more difficult that you might think. Player one simply begins by saying a county, i.e. **Devon**, and play continues until a player either cannot think of a new county or says a county that has already been mentioned. The **usual fine** applies to the loser.

Um, States

Like **States** before it, **Um, States** is a simple game of territory-naming that works best if played with people that don't know the following important rule. It is this: play moves around the circle naming US states, but to get your guess right, you have to add an **"um"** before you mention the name of the state in question. If you don't use the **"um"**,

Hints & Tips
Swotty, boring types may want to gen up on the names of all the states.
Let them do it, but don't let them ever play again...

you are not aware of the pattern and must drink a forfeit. In this game, players that know the pattern can repeat states as long as they use an **"um"** or make up new states. Anything goes as long as there's an **"um"**. Play ends when the players who didn't know the rules to begin with, finally crack the pattern.

Scissors States
Like **Um, States,** but instead of adding the word **"um"** in front of the name of the state concerned, you say the name of the state (or a made up area) with your arms casually crossed. Anybody who doesn't know the rules, has to drink. Ha-ha.

Bolloxed factor...

BOUNCING BALL

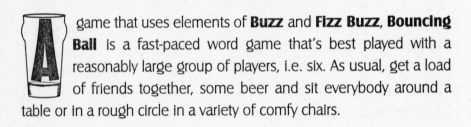

⚠️ **A GAME PLAYED WITH AN INVISIBLE BALL. YET AFTER 16 PINTS, YOU MIGHT BE ABLE TO SEE IT!**

ESSENTIAL SUPPLIES
Beer. Spirits. An imaginary ball.

 game that uses elements of **Buzz** and **Fizz Buzz**, **Bouncing Ball** is a fast-paced word game that's best played with a reasonably large group of players, i.e. six. As usual, get a load of friends together, some beer and sit everybody around a table or in a rough circle in a variety of comfy chairs.

The basic rule of the game is this: only three words can be spoken once the game begins – **"Whizz"**, **"Bounce"**, and **"Boing"**. Next, pick somebody to start the game. This person holds the imaginary ball which will move around the group depending on which of the three words the players say.

If a player says **"Whizz"** the ball passes on to the next player.

If a player says **"Bounce"**, the ball skips the next player and bounces on to the following player.

Finally, if a player says **"Boing"**, the ball reverses direction.

So in a sample game, it would work like this. Play begins with player

Hints & Tips
As with any of the word games in this chapter, the faster you play this game, the more fun you'll be certain to have.

one who says **"Whizz"**; player two gets the ball and says **"Boing"** sending it back to player one; player one now gets the ball and says **"Boing"** to send the ball back to player two; player two says **"Whizz"** to give it to player three; player three says **"Bounce"** to skip player four and move onto player one. And so on. Drinking penalties are incurred if any player hesitates, or says a word when he/she doesn't have the ball or passes the ball the wrong way.

Bolloxed factor...

IBBLE DIBBLE

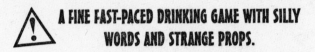

⚠ **A FINE FAST-PACED DRINKING GAME WITH SILLY WORDS AND STRANGE PROPS.**

ESSENTIAL SUPPLIES
Beer. Spirits. A cork. A lighter (or box of matches)

rrange a gang of players around a table, and assign each one of these players **a number**. So, assuming there are four players, assign numbers **1-4** to the people around the table in a clockwise direction.

Make sure everybody has at least one large drink, then take the cork and blacken one end of it by burning it with the lighter or the matches. **Now for the game...** First of all, it's vital that you understand these two basic concepts – an **"ibble dibble"** is a player who wants to get drunk; a **"dibble ibble"** is a black mark on a players face made by the cork. Once you understand this, you can start to play the game.

Whoever has been assigned the number **1** kicks off the game and can pass the play onto anybody else in the circle by **naming himself** (i.e. **"number 1 ibble-dibble"** – player one who wants to get drunk), **identifying how many marks he has** ("with no dibble-ibbles" – no cork marks), and then **calling another player and identifying the number of marks they have ("calling number 3 ibble-dibble with 1 dibble-ibble"** – player three who wants to get drunk and has no marks).

So, a sample game might go something like this: player one says: "This is number 1 **ibble-dibble** with no **dibble-ibbles** calling number 3

Hints & Tips

Try not to have too far to travel home after you've been playing this.
No cab is going to stop for someone covered in dibble-ibbles.

ibble-dibble with no **dibble-ibbles**"; player three would then quickly respond with: "This is number 3 **ibble-dibble** with no **dibble-ibbles** calling number 4 **ibble-dibble** with no **dibble-ibbles**". If player three had paused, he/she would have a sooty mark added to their face and has to drink a penalty. Then the player can continue; "This is number 3 **ibble- dibble** with 1 **dibble-ibble** calling number 2 **ibble-dibble** with no **dibble-ibbles**". And so on. Drinking penalties are incurred for hesitation, or for getting your number of marks (**dibble-ibbles**) wrong, or for getting your **dibble-ibbles** and your **ibble-dibbles** mixed up.

Bolloxed factor...

CHEERS!

ANIMAL

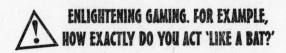

⚠️ **ENLIGHTENING GAMING. FOR EXAMPLE, HOW EXACTLY DO YOU ACT 'LIKE A BAT?'**

ESSENTIAL SUPPLIES
Beer. Spirits.

With a group of friends sat around a table, encourage each potential player to think of an animal, plus a noise and an action that will define that animal to the other players – i.e. a snake might be a hiss and a stuck-out tongue; a monkey might be a screech, illustrated by a player banging their fists on their chest.

To play the game, make sure that all of the players know what animals the others have chosen and pick a player to start. This player then makes their distinctive animal action and the accompanying noise, then the action and noise of another player's animal. This next player then performs their animal action and noise, plus that of another player in the circle. This continues around the circle. Drinking penalties are incurred if a player hesitates or if players get another player's animal action or noise incorrect.

 Hints & Tips

Once again, the faster you play this game, the better. Expect other people in the pub to be highly amused, as well.

Bolloxed factor...

🍾🍾🍾🍾🍾🍾🍾🍾

BERNARD

⚠ **A GAME THAT GETS A REALLY GOOD RESPONSE IF THERE'S A BERNARD IN THE ROOM...**

ESSENTIAL SUPPLIES
Beer. Spirits.

Oh-so-simple, **Bernard** isn't really a game, it's more of an arrogant **'event'** (if you're taking part) and an annoyance (if you're sat in the pub while a group of tanked-up lads are playing it). Best played outside or in the confines of your own house, **Bernard** is a vocal game in which you sit/stand in a rough circle and the first person whispers the name **'Bernard'**. Then the next person in the circle has to say **'Bernard'**, but in a slightly louder voice, as does the next person. The increasingly loud spouting of **Bernard** continues round the group until the participants are shouting **Bernard** at the top of their voices. The player who doesn't shout **'Bernard'** louder than the previous player is the loser and must drink an entire pint while the others ritually chant **'Bernard, Bernard, Bernard'**.

Variants:

Don't just stick to **Bernard.** North London football fans might want to try yelling **'Arsenal'**; English students could yell **'Postmodernism'**; drunken louts might even wish to yell obscenities.

Hints & Tips

It sounds like a terrible game and it is. Unless you're the one playing it. Watch the pub empty as soon as you start.

Bolloxed factor...

🍾🍾🍾🍾🍾🍾🍾🍾

GOING TO THE BEACH

⚠ **DON'T WORRY, YOU DON'T ACTUALLY GO TO THE BEACH IN THIS GAME....**

ESSENTIAL SUPPLIES
Beer. Spirits.

nother one of those drinking games that rely on a **secret system** that at least half of the players aren't aware of. Best played with **a large group** of players (let's say six is optimum), the players sit in a circle and nominate a player to **'go to the beach'**. This player then starts the game, a light-hearted memory diversion, by announcing: **"I'm going to the beach and I'm taking..."** plus the name of an item that starts with their first initial. For example, Steve might say "I'm going to the beach and I'm taking Sardines"; and John could opt for: "I'm going to the beach and I'm taking some jam." If Bill chips in with "I'm going to the beach and I'm taking some peanuts", then he is wrong, everybody tuts and shakes their heads, and forces the unfortunate bloke to drink a **two-finger/sip penalty**. Repeat until the new players have discovered the secret system and it's no longer fun.

Variants: The Name Game
Similar to **Going To The Beach**, this game is played using the same system, but structured around questions, the answers to which are always two words starting with the player's initials. So, if members of **Arsenal's** 1998 title-winning team were playing, the game would progress as follows: if the question asked is "What hobby do you

Hints & Tips

If nobody else knows the secret of the game, you might have to tip a couple of people off before you start playing it.

have?", **Dennis Bergkamp** would respond with: **'Diving Backwards'**; **Nicolas Anelka** would say: **"Nut Augmentation"**, **Martin Keown** would quip: **'Making Kettles'**. Sounds simple, but there should be a strict time limit and anybody who fails to think of a two-word answer in, say, **ten seconds**, incurs the boozy penalty.

Bolloxed factor...

CHEERS!

GUESS THE NOTE

 WHAT'S THE BET THAT THIS GAME IS ALL THE RAGE AT MUSIC SCHOOLS?

ESSENTIAL SUPPLIES
Bottled beer. Musical instruments.

game for the musically inclined, **Guess The Note** works best with a piano, but does work reasonably well with a guitar. To play: one player sits down with the instrument in question, while the others drink some of the beer from the bottles so that each one is left with a different level of beer remaining. Then, in turn, the players with the beer bottles blow notes on their impromptu instruments. The player at the piano/with the guitar, then gets **three chances** to try and emulate the note on his/her instrument. If the player manages to repeat the note, then the other players must drink the remaining beer. But if the player can't, he/she must drink the remaining beer.

Hints & Tips
The game can also be played with your favourite records.
Simply choose a distinct moment from a track...

Bolloxed factor...

SEX AND DRUGS AND ROCK 'N' ROLL

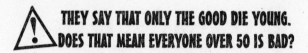

⚠️ **THEY SAY THAT ONLY THE GOOD DIE YOUNG. DOES THAT MEAN EVERYONE OVER 50 IS BAD?**

ESSENTIAL SUPPLIES
Beer. Spirits.

Gather a group of friends together, give everybody lots of beer and nominate a player to go first. That player must then pick a letter from the alphabet, say **'C'**, and the player must think of a word starting with this letter that is related to either sex, drugs or rock 'n' roll. For example, if player one picked **'C'**, they could say **'Condom'**. Player two would then have to think of a word beginning with **'D'**, player three with **'E'** and so on. When a player cannot think of a suitable word, he/she must drink **half-a-pint** for every minute that they spend thinking. Drinking penalties are also incurred for made-up words, unsuitable words (the validity of dodgy words can be voted on by the other players) and for passing on letters (i.e. **X**). Play continues for as long as you find it interesting.

Hints & Tips
Unless you want to ban swearing, you'll find that this is a fairly obscene-sounding game. Not for kindergarten.

Bolloxed factor...

HANDS UP, HANDS DOWN

⚠️ **A TEAM GAME OF MISDIRECTION, SHOUTING AND TOUCHING HANDS UNDER TABLES.**

ESSENTIAL SUPPLIES
Beer. Spirits. A coin.

This game requires the participation of two teams, sitting or standing, and across from each other with a table between them. Each team must also consist of at least three players. One team holds their hands face up in the air, about chest level. One of this team's members is holding a coin that's visible to both teams.

When a player on the opposing team (the announcer) yells **"Hands down!"**, the team with the coin thrust their hands underneath the table, where team members can secretly pass it between each other, hoping to fool the other team in the same way a street-hawker plays with a pea and three cups.

After a random amount of time (determined by the announcer on the opposite team), the announcer yells **"Hands up!"** and the coin-holding team, clench their fists (one of them holding the coin) and return them to their original, chest-height position. Then the announcer on the opposite team yells **"Hands down!"** again and, in unison and while shouting **"haa!!"** (to mask the sound of the coin), the coin-holders slam both of their hands down on the table, palms down,

Hints & Tips

Try and use a reasonably large and heavy coin, so that it's not fumbled easily – a 50p-piece is probably the best option.

concealing the coin from the opposition. Now, starting from the right, the opposite team must attempt to guess which hand the coin is in by touching one of the opposing teams' hands. The person touched must then open his hand and reveal the contents. If the opposing team finds the coin, the coin-holding team takes a drink. If they don't, everyone on the guessing team drinks.

Bolloxed factor...

CHEERS!

TAILS

 YOU'D THINK THAT TAILS WAS A GAME WITH MONEY. BUT YOU'D BE WRONG.

ESSENTIAL SUPPLIES
Beer. Spirits.

As usual, for this fast-paced game, gather a group of friends together in a circle or around a table, and select one of the players to go first. This player can then either say **"Tails to the left X"** or **"Tails to the right X"** (where X is a number between 1 and 5).

If the player says "Tails to the right 3", then the player who is sitting three seats away on the right of the calling player has to respond with a **"Tails to the..."** shout of their own.

Players that **hesitate** too long, must drink. Anybody who gets caught with a drinking penalty three times in a row must drink the contents of a whole pint.

 Hints & Tips
To make the game more fun, see if you can find a "tail" to wave when it's your go; feather boas are great.

Bolloxed factor...

178

CAPTAIN BLUFF

⚠ OFTEN CONFUSED WITH CAPTAIN SNUFF. BUT THAT'S SOMETHING COMPLETELY DIFFERENT.

ESSENTIAL SUPPLIES
Beer. Spirits.

Again the ingredients are: a group of friends, beer and a table. Nominate a player to be the first **Captain Bluff**. This player then starts the game by saying: **"Captain Bluff takes his first drink."** After this the player picks up his beer with one finger and thumb, takes one sip, places the beer back on the table, tapping it once, winks once, pinches his left ear with his left hand once, his right ear with his right hand once, stands up and turns around once, before sitting down again. The other players must repeat this procedure exactly.

If everyone succeeds, **Captain Bluff** then announces: **"Captain Bluff takes his second drink"**, following this with another suitably strange collection of gestures which the players must then repeat. Anybody who fails, gets a drinking penalty and must try to emulate **Captain Bluff**'s movements again.

Hints & Tips
If Captain Bluff loses track of what he's done, it's time for a new Captain. "Mutiny, Mr Christian?" Too right.

Bolloxed factor...

179

WALES TALES

⚠ READ IT THROUGH TWICE. THEN YOU'LL UNDERSTAND IT.

ESSENTIAL SUPPLIES
Beer. Spirits.

Right. Listen closely. Because the rules can get quite complicated. As usual get a group of people together and form everybody into a standing circle, with one player nominated as the **Prince Of Wales** – obviously if the real **Prince Of Wales** is playing with you, it's a good idea to pick him.

Whoever is chosen, the newly-dubbed Prince calls out: **"Wales tales, the Prince of Wales calls tales, on a court of 4 on X"**.

What it all means is this: the **'tales'** refer to how the players are designated in the circle. For example, **"Regular Tales"** means that players in the circle are numbered 1, 2, 3 ,4 etc. with 1 being the Prince Of Wales; **"Greek Tales"** means that the players are numbered Alpha, Beta, Gamma, Delta, etc.; **"French Tales"** means the numbers are in French – Un, Deux, Trois, Quatre, and so on.

The **'court of'** is the number of people playing the game – court size of 4 equals 4 players. While **'on X'** refers to the starting player, where X is the number of the player counted clockwise away from the Prince.

A sample game might look like this. Player A calls: **"Wales tales, the Prince of Wales calls Regular Tales, on a court of 4 on 2"**. The players sit in a rough circle (shown below), **'Regular Tales'** means players A, B, C and D will have to use normal numbers; while **'on a**

180

Hints & Tips
When it's your turn to choose a number, be careful that you don't accidentally pick yourself again. You'll never live it down.

court of 4 on 2' means that four people are playing and play will continue with the player two seats away from the Prince.

A

D B

C

In this case, the '4 on 2' means that the Prince has picked the player two seats away (i.e. player C) and this player must quickly respond with **"Nay"**. To this, the Prince responds **"Who?"** which leads to the picked player (still C) choosing another player to transfer the play to. He/she does this by saying a number between 1 and 4 (the court size) which is the number of seats that the new player is away from them. Confused? Try this:

Player A: "Wales Tales, the Prince Of Wales, calls Greek rotational tales, on a court of Delta on Beta."

(play moves two seats clockwise to player C)
Player C: "nay"

Player A: "who"
Player C: "Gamma"
(play moves three seats clockwise to player B)
Player B: "nay"
Player C: "who"
Player B: "Alpha"
(play moves one seat clockwise to player C)
And so on...

The rotation of play can be altered (**Regular, Reverse,** etc.) and new tales can be added where appropriate. As in most word-based drinking games, penalties are incurred for hesitation and incorrect answers.

Bolloxed factor...

CLAP-SLAP

 SOUNDS LIKE A DANGEROUS SEXUAL DISEASE. THANKFULLY IT ISN'T.

ESSENTIAL SUPPLIES
Beer. Spirits.

If you think you remember this game from your childhood, you're probably right. It's an old game, a kid's game, but now reinvented with an adult twist. Simply gather a group of friends into a circle and begin clapping slowly, in unison, using the following method: **(1)** slap your legs with both hands, **(2)** then clap both hands, before **(3)** clicking your fingers on both hands. The game itself is one of those initially simple, then devilishly cunning entertainments. Nominate a player to go first. This player then calls out **'Names Of'** ('Names' is called on the thigh-slapping phase, 'Of' is called during the clap phase), then a category of no more than two syllables – cars, planes, etc. Play then proceeds clockwise. Like the **'Names Of'** call, answers can only be called out a syllable at a time and only during the slap and clap phases (hence the name of the game). For example: if the category is **'women'**, players can use the slap-clap rhythm to answer with Mich-elle, or Ja-net, or Con-nie, and so on. If players say a word that does not fit the rhythm or falls out of step with the slapping, clapping and clicking, then the usual drinking fine applies.

Hints & Tips
Do NOT start playing the game proper unless the group has something approaching a decent rhythm.

Bolloxed factor...

SERGEANT MAJOR GENERAL

⚠ **A FAST-PACED, NAME-CALLING GAME WITH A MACHO MILITARY THEME.**

ESSENTIAL SUPPLIES
Beer. Spirits.

nother simple word game which involves calling people names for amusement. Specifically, once you've gathered a sizable group of friends around (say about six), these players are given ranks. Nominate a starting player and, moving clockwise around the group, dub player 1 the **'General'**, player 2 the **'Major'**, player 3 the **'Sergeant'**, player 4 **'1'**, player 5 **'2'**, and player 6 the **'Dunce'**. The game is kicked off by the General who calls out his own rank, followed by the rank of another player. I.e. General 1, or General Major. Quickly, the player referenced in the previous player's call must pass the play onwards by calling out their own rank followed by somebody else's number. For example:

The General: General 1
Player 1: 1 Major
The Major: Major Sergeant
And so on...

The only real rule is that the game cannot be passed onto a player that is (a) sat either side of the caller, or (b) to the player that just gave the

Hints & Tips

Try and decide what you're going to say before your rank is called out. Boy scouts should find this game particularly easy.

game to you. Anybody who speaks at the wrong time, or hesitates when called, drinks an appropriate forfeit. This loser then becomes the **Dunce** who must sit in the **Dunce's seat**, and the rest of the players swap seats and ranks accordingly.

Bolloxed factor...

CHEERS!

SPOOKS

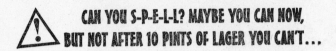

**CAN YOU S-P-E-L-L? MAYBE YOU CAN NOW,
BUT NOT AFTER 10 PINTS OF LAGER YOU CAN'T...**

ESSENTIAL SUPPLIES
Beer. Spirits.

Like **Sentences** in this chapter, **Spooks** is a word game where the object is to say as many letters as you can without making a word. Gather that familiar group of friends together and nominate one of your number to go first. The designated player 1 then thinks of a word and, without telling anybody what it is, offers up the first letter. The other players then add subsequent letters to the evolving word, trying not to be the one that finishes the word. For example, (in a four-player game) if player one thinks of the word 'Promise', he/she will say 'P' as the first letter of the word. Player two does not know what the original word is, so he/she might then add an 'A', Player three can't add a 'D', 'L', or an 'N' because that would make a word, so bolts on a 'G' to make PAG. Player four then adds an 'I' thinking of 'Paging', Player one is restricted in his choice of letters but can't get caught out and adds a condemning 'N' to make PAGIN. Player two, unfortunately, is stuffed. A 'G' is the obvious letter, but that ends the word and the game, making player two the loser. The penalty, of course, is a swift drink. Alco-fines are also incurred for **hesitation** and adding letters that the other players challenge. If a word cannot be formed, the last player to add a letter, must drink.

Hints & Tips
As you can tell from the example, words quickly form.
Player two has overlooked 'pagination' however.

Bolloxed factor...

LIKE PISSED

⚠️ **IT DOESN'T GET ANY SIMPLER AND WILDER THAN THIS.**

ESSENTIAL SUPPLIES
Beer. Spirits.

Like **Pissed** is a simple, one-off game of no real skill whatsoever. What it relies on is the players' knowledge of words that mean **'drunk'**. Gather your favourite drinking partners together around a table and then, with drinks in hand, take it in turn to name a word or phrase that is a slang synonym for inebriation. We've listed some examples below:

Shedded, Slaughtered, Bladdered, Tanked, Rat-arsed, Under The Table, Shit faced, Had One Too Many, Merry, Tipsy, Intoxicated, Boozed up, Seeing Double, Wasted, Slammed, Off Yer Trolley, Half-Cut, Squiffy, Plastered, Sozzled, Sloshed, Screwed, Oiled, Beered Up, Lagered Up, Blind drunk, Three Sheets In The Wind, Drunk As A Lord, Ripped, Trashed, Hammered, Skunked, Gooned, Pissed Out Of Your Tree, Sauced, Loaded, Annihilated, Bolloxed... and so on.

Anybody who can't think of a word or phrase, must drink the usual **forfeit**. If any player offers a word that the others challenge, the group can put it to a **vote** to decide its validity

Hints & Tips
This game won't last forever, so have another one ready and prepared for when it all starts to peter out...

Bolloxed factor...
🍾🍾🍾🍾🍾🍾🍾🍾

187

CHAPTER 6

TV, MOVIE AND SPORT-BASED GAMES

Like their card, dice and coin-based cousins, drinking games based on TV shows, movies or sports rely on the random element to dish out the beer-related penalties. And in every instance below, the rules are the same. Check the Essential supplies to see exactly what you'll need for a **Red Dwarf** night or a **Star Wars** evening, pick a character (if told to do so) and simply drink when an action or a quote appears in the lists here. That's all there is to it. Adding a drinking element to some of your favourite shows, gives the night a refreshing, woozy twist. Now you don't have to blame your friends for urging you to have another pint, you can blame C3-PO for saying that he's familiar with over six million forms of communication; or condemn Liverpool's Michael Owen for getting far too much of the ball. Whichever game you play, we've scoured the Earth to bring you the best in media-based drinking games.

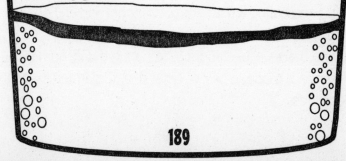

THE RED DWARF
DRINKING GAME

⚠️ **ALCOHOL MEETS LISTER, RIMMER, CAT AND KRYTEN IN THIS BOOZY DRINK-A-THON.**

ESSENTIAL SUPPLIES
Red Dwarf videos. Beer or spirits.

Pop a whole series of **Red Dwarf** on the TV, sit back and take a swig from your bottle of beer when any of the following happen on the screen. For best effect, and if there are a group of you, pick one of the main characters (i.e. Lister, Kryten, Rimmer, The Cat, or Kochanksi) and watch closely for any of that character's actions on-screen. If you see, for example, **Lister** having a lager and you have chosen **Lister**, then take a drink.

If you picked Lister, take a drink every time that:
- Lister has a Lager.
- He refers to an old lover (drink double if he does this especially to make Rimmer feel bad).
- He mentions Kristine Kochanski.
- Lister is seen eating a curry (or other gooey Indian Food).
- Lister plays his guitar.
- Someone makes a joke about Lister being barely human.
- A reference is made to any of Lister's undergarments and their state of cleanliness.

• Lister enters an artificial reality computer game. Double if he does so to have sex.

If you picked Rimmer, take a drink every time that:
• Someone insults Rimmer.
• He insults someone back, or just insults someone for the hell of it.
• Rimmer does something mean to someone else.
• An embarrassing fact is revealed about his character, his childhood, his love-life and especially if anybody mentions his middle name.
• Rimmer mentions one of his dull hobbies or interests (such extracurricular oddities include Risk, Hammond Organs, 20th Century Telegraph poles, etc.)
• Rimmer has a whinge about being dead – this only really applies to series 1 and 2 of the show.
• Rimmer tells of his love for military battles or mentions a great general.
• Rimmer misquotes a Space Corp Directive.
• Rimmer thinks that aliens exist or that they are nearby.
• Ace Rimmer says: "Smoke me a kipper, I'll be back for breakfast!"
• Lister calls Ace Rimmer "Skipper".
• Anyone says "What a guy!" about Ace Rimmer.

If you picked Cat, take a drink every time that:
• The Cat mentions an "old cat saying".

(continued overleaf)

- The Cat mention his favourite pastimes (like: sex, food, sleep, etc.)
- The Cat goes "Aaaooooww!"
- The Cat wants to go out with any woman that the others have mentioned or that they come across in their travels.
- The Cat praises his own good looks, or looks in the mirror. Drink double if he claims to be centre of the universe.
- The Cat changes costume.
- Duane Dibley appears. In fact, Drink triple.
- The Cat 'smells' something, or his sense of smell is referred to by another crew member. Double if he mentions that his nostril hairs are vibrating.

If you picked Kryten, take a drink every time that:
- Kryten has to explain something technological to another member of the crew.
- He is seen ironing, cooking or doing the laundry.
- Kryten's head is described in an amusing way by a member of the crew (e.g. "amusingly shaped ice-cube")
- He corrects a Space Corp Directive quoted by Rimmer.
- An add-on appliance for his body is mentioned in conversation or seen in the episode. Drink double if he ever recounts a tale about an accident with his groinal socket or groinal attachment.
- Kryten comes up with an "old android saying".
- He speaks something in binary or hex.
- He offers to kill himself for doing something stupid or as a sacrifice to save the crew.
- He enters an android mode, such as "smug mode" or "lie mode".

If you picked Kochanski, take a drink every time that:
- She complains about being in a parallel universe, or complains about the food or complains about Lister's dirty habits.

- Lister tries to make a pass at her and she shoots him down in flames (metaphorically speaking).
- She is seen wearing that tight red rubber outfit. Mmmm...
- The Cat calls her "officer-bud-babe".
- She is sarcastic or makes a snooty comment in a desperate situation where everybody's lives are in mortal peril.
- She refers to "Her Dave".

Bonus drinking. Take a swig every time that any of the following happen:

- Holly is stupid.
- Holly has troubles with numbers or just with counting from 1-10, or from 10-1 to be exact.
- Holly uses a pop culture word, like "Dude" and "Oi!".
- Holly makes a reference to his/her IQ, or lack of it.
- Holly's head appears on something other than a TV screen on a wall – i.e. Lister's watch, Kryten's stomach. It does happen.
- A Skutter is seen on the screen.
- The Skutters play Cowboys and Indians or show that they are John Wayne fans.
- The Skutters annoy Rimmer.
- The Talkie Toaster offers anyone a slice of toast.
- The Talkie Toaster offers anyone another type of toasted product.
- The Polymorph changes into a new, disgusting and/or salivating monster.
- Someone says "Red Dwarf".
- The theme song is played or heard in the background. This rule is best expanded to include songs and singing of all kinds including the "I'm gonna eat you little fishy" and the "Ohm" ditties.
- Somebody mentions a small, furry animal or a kipper.
- An alien they meet wants to kill them. (continued overleaf)

- The aliens that want to kill them can't shoot straight.
- The crew parody something from another sci-fi show.
- Somebody says "smeg", "smegging", "smeghead".

Bolloxed factor...

THE STAR WARS TRILOGY

DRINKING GAME.

⚠ **RUMOUR HAD THAT OBI-WAN KENOBI COULD DRINK 10 PINTS OF TATTOOINE ALE A NIGHT...**

ESSENTIAL SUPPLIES
Star Wars, The Empire Strikes Back, Return Of The Jedi. Beer. Lots of free time.

As usual, watch either **Star Wars**, **The Empire Strikes Back** or **Return Of The Jedi** and take a good old swig from your beer when any of the following happen on the screen.

• Someone has a bad feeling about this.
• It's their only hope.
• An entire planet is described as having one climate.
• Somebody gets choked.
• A woman other than Leia is on screen.
• An old Jedi starts to ramble about the Force.
• Somebody's hand/arm gets cut off.
• There is a tremor in the Force.
• It's not someone's fault.
• One or more heroes are almost eaten by a large alien 'thing'.
• Someone exclaims "No!"
• Someone wears the same outfit in all three movies.
• Someone is mind-controlled using the Force.
• A good guy wears white/ a bad guy wears black. (continued overleaf)

- An alien character has lines in its original language (with or without subtitles).
- A spacecraft crashes into something after being hit by laser fire.
- A light sabre is used.
- An Ewok dies, and the camera lingers on it for dramatic effect.
- Luke whines.
- Luke fights monsters or savages.
- Luke performs an impossible acrobatic tumble/flip.
- Luke is upside-down.
- Luke and Lando are onscreen at the same time.
- Luke refuses to take someone's advice.
- Leia insults somebody.
- Leia wears an outfit that covers everything except her face and hands.
- A see-through Obi-Wan Kenobi appears to offer advice.
- Han boasts about the capabilities of the Millennium Falcon.
- Somebody insults the capabilities of the Millennium Falcon.
- Despite its capabilities, something doesn't work on the Millennium Falcon.
- C3-PO loses a body part.
- C3-PO brags how many forms of communication he's familiar with.
- A Rebel Pilot says "Nice Shot..."
- A Rebel Pilot says "I've been hit..."
- Any Imperial Ship is destroyed.
- A Rebel ship is destroyed.
- Grand Moff Tarkin boasts about the awesome capabilities of the Death Star.
- The Emperor cackles evilly.
- The Emperor has foreseen something.
- The Emperor fires lightning bolts from his hands (keep drinking while the lightning continues).
- Boba Fett speaks.

• A Stormtrooper, despite the fact that he's wearing body armour, gets hit once by a laser blast and dies. Drink twice if he falls from a high place.

Bolloxed factor...

CHEERS!

THE X-FILES
DRINKING GAME

⚠️ **SO MANY CLICHES, SO LITTLE TIME. JOIN MILDER AND SCULLY FOR AN EPISODE OF THE XXXX-FILES.**

ESSENTIAL SUPPLIES
As many episodes of the spooky TV series as you can find. Beer.

ou know the drill by now... Pop an episode into the video (the ones that feature the alien subplot are particularly effective) and take a drink every time one of the following events occur.

Take one swig from your drink when:

• Scully is called to do a post-mortem or examines a corpse.

• Mulder or Scully gets a call on their mobile phones from their partner.

• A powerful torch is waved in a very dark, slightly dusty room.

• Mulder mentions that something could be alien/paranormal/mystical etc. and another character thinks he's joking.

• Mulder mentions that something could be alien/paranormal/mystical etc. and Scully counters with a scientific explanation.

• Mulder mentions an old case with a similar theme that's almost directly related to the case that they're working on.

• Mulder and Scully split up to follow separate leads. Scully's lead proves to be a waste of time and she misses the alien/paranormal finale and doesn't believe Mulder when he tells her about it.

• A mysterious character shows up at the end of an episode to keep Mulder from learning the truth.

• A mysterious character shows up at the end of an episode to save Mulder's life.

Take two swigs from your drink when:

- Someone knows something about Mulder's sister. But they won't tell him about it.
- You spot the numbers 11/21, which correspond to the birthday of Chris Carter's wife...
- Mulder is called by his first name, Fox.
- Cancer Man lights a cigarette.
- Mulder mentions that his sister was abducted when he was very young.
- Someone calls Mulder "Spooky Mulder."
- Deep Throat or Mr. X appears, complains that they should stop meeting like this, and tells Mulder absolutely nothing of importance.
- Mulder and Scully get into a fight.

Take three swigs from your drink when:

- A UFO appears or something paranormal happens in Scully's presence and she finds it difficult to explain.
- Scully ventures into dark place on her own.
- An alien appears (dead, frozen, running around, etc.)
- The shapeshifting aliens appear.
- Someone brandishes one of those retractable ice picks.
- A local Sheriff helps the FBI in their investigation.

(continued overleaf)

Then there's the much, much shorter X-Files Drinking Game. Which goes like so:

- Mulder or Scully uses a flashlight (1 finger/sip)
- Mulder or Scully shows a badge and says "FBI" (1 finger/sip)
- Mulder gets in a fist fight (1 finger/sip)
- An alien appears (1 finger/sip)
- Cancer Man appears (2 fingers/sips)
- Mulder thinks about or makes reference to his sister (2 fingers/sips)
- Someone says "The Truth is Out There" (2 fingers/sips)
- Scully is called away before the climax and therefore misses the overwhelming evidence that aliens/ghosts/large man worms/witchcraft etc. exists. (3 fingers/sips)

Bolloxed factor...

THE ROXANNE

DRINKING GAME

⚠ **YOU WOULDN'T THINK THAT A THREE MINUTE SONG COULD GET YOU PLASTERED. BUT YOU'D BE WRONG...**

ESSENTIAL SUPPLIES
A copy of The Police's famous song, Roxanne. Beer.

Oh-so-simple, yet oh-so-deadly. Dig up a copy of **The Police** tune **Roxanne**, bung it on the record player or in your CD system (or on the jukebox in your local) and drink every time you hear the band sing **'Roxanne'**. Surprisingly, that's all there is to it. We guarantee you'll be amazed at how many times the word **'Roxanne'** actually turns up. It's a hell of a lot.

Hints & Tips
This admirable game can be easily converted to other songs. "War", "Delilah", "Pump up the volume". etc. etc...

Bolloxed factor...
🍾🍾🍾🍾🍾🍾🍾🍾🍾

THE SMURFS
DRINKING GAME

⚠️ **YES. WATCHING THE INNOCENT, BLUE 'TOONS WITH THE FUNNY HATS DOES MAKE A GOOD DRINKING GAME...**

ESSENTIAL SUPPLIES
The Smurf's TV show. Beer.

Here's how it works, watch any repeat of the **Smurfs** (or just come across it by accident on a kids satellite/cable channel) and drink yourself into oblivion courtesy of Papa Smurf, Hefty Smurf and Smurfette. The rules are laughably simple but fiendishly precise: knock back two fingers/sips of beer every time that one of the small, blue abominations says **"Smurf"**. For some deadlier danger, drink double (4 fingers) every time a Smurf says **"Papa Smurf"** and triple (6 fingers) every time that somebody mentions Smurfette. Drink quadruple the penalty if the evil wizard Gargamel appears and he fails, in an inept slapstick way, to catch any of the **Smurfs** he's chasing. Drink your whole drink if Gargamel conveniently forgets where the Smurf village is at the end of the episode.

Variants:The Teletubbies
Although there's something distinctly dirty about mutating a kid's TV show into a vehicle for regular and prolonged alcohol abuse, if you've done it with the **Smurfs**, you might as well try it with Britain's most recent, mind-numbing creation, **The Teletubbies**. If you can bear it, watch an episode of this bright, cuddly show and drink every time that **(a)** the heroes sing and **(b)**, La La, Tinky Winky, Dipsy or Po is mentioned by name. For a Russian Roulette angle to the kiddy

proceedings, pay with four players and before the programme starts, pick a Teletubby character each. Then, when it gets to that tense point in the show where the podgy, multi-coloured protagonists show TV clips on their stomachs, the drinker whose character is chosen to broadcast the TV signals, must down his/her entire pint in one go.

Bolloxed factor...

CHEERS!

THE JAMES BOND
DRINKING GAME

 ANOTHER SIMPLE GAME – EASY ON THE BRAIN, HEAVY ON THE BEER.

ESSENTIAL SUPPLIES
Any of the 18 James Bond films on video. Beer.

op any one of the 18 **James Bond** movies into your video and start watching. The rules, such as they are here, are ludicrously simple: every time that a character in the movie says **"James"**, drink twice from your beverage of choice; every time that a character in the movie says **"Bond"**, sip three times from your drink. Finally every time that someone says **"James Bond"**, drink half of your drink in one go and cheer happily. Like the **Roxanne** drinking game, the idea behind this alcoholic Bondage is fairly straightforward, but you'll be surprised how many times that 007's name will crop up. Watch out for the megalomaniac villains, who revel in saying "Bond" more times than most, and the drop-their- dresses-on-the-floor girls who whisper "Oh, James" before being relegated to a plot device. Try it for yourself and see how you go.

 ## Hints & Tips
You can always drink dry vodka martinis, prepared in that special way, if you want a little bit more authenticity.

Bolloxed factor...

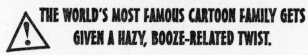

THE SIMPSONS
DRINKING GAMES
1 AND 2

⚠ **THE WORLD'S MOST FAMOUS CARTOON FAMILY GETS GIVEN A HAZY, BOOZE-RELATED TWIST.**

ESSENTIAL SUPPLIES
A vast haul of Simpsons episodes on tape. Beer.

There are two versions of **The Simpsons Drinking Game** – the first is based on a large group picking a character each and then watching several episodes back-to-back. While the second is a much more general game, a collection of popular Simpsons-isms that can be combined with drinking penalties to make an enjoyable and brain-slowing game. First up, though, is **The Simpsons Drinking Game 1** – pick a character from the show and quickly imbibe some alcohol if your character gets caught doing any following actions:

Homer Simpson
- Says "Doh!" (drink twice if somebody else uses his famous catchphrase).
- Eats donuts, talks about donuts, sees donuts, dreams about donuts.
- Drools uncontrollably.
- Has a conversation with his own brain.
- Drinks some Duff beer.

Lisa Simpson
- Mentions humanity, the environment, truth, justice or (continued overleaf)

the American way.
- Reads Junior Sceptic magazine.
- Plays the saxophone.

Bart Simpson
- Makes a crank phone call to Moe.
- Says "Aye Carumba!"
- Wears something other than his usual top and shorts.

Marge Simpson
- Her towering blue hair casts a giant shadow.
- She says "Homey".
- She kisses Homer.
- She growls at Homer.
- She makes the family tea and defends her husband.

Maggie Simpson
- She falls down.
- She removes her dummy for a moment.
- Says a word (drink your whole pint if this happens, plus all of the beer you have in the house!)

Marge's sisters
- If they appear in a scene together (drink triple if one of them appears on their own).
- They smoke.
- They criticise Homer.

Ned Flanders:
- Mentions God, Religion, the Church or says "Okely-Dokely".

Now, cue **The Simpson's Drinking Game 2** – a more general game which can be played by any number of Simpsons fans. Simply consult the handy table below, which lists the various onscreen actions and the drinking penalties that they incur:

- Pets make an appearance (1 finger/sip)
- Barney Drinks (1 finger/sip)
- Springfield Police corruption is revealed or the bumbling cops fail to catch a criminal (1 finger/sip)
- Homer eats a donut (1 finger/sip)
- Dr. Hibbert laughs (1 finger/sip)
- Troy McLure says "Hi, I'm Troy McLure" (1 finger/sip)
- Bart rides his skateboard (1 finger/sip)
- Flanders says "Hidely-ho neighbor" (1 finger/sip)
- Patty/Selma light a cigarette (1 finger/sip)
- Nelson says "Haah-haah" (1 finger/sip)
- Evil nuclear power plant boss Mr. Burns says, "excellent" (1 finger/sip)
- Any Flanders member makes a reference to God (1 finger/sip)
- Grampa talks about "Matlock" (1 finger/sip)
- There's a serious alert at the Nuclear Plant (1 finger/sip)
- Homer tries another job (1 finger/sip)
- Maggie shares a pacifier (2 fingers/sips)
- Marge puts or takes something out of her hair (2 fingers/sip)
- Smithers makes a sexual reference toward Mr. Burns (3 fingers/sips).

Bolloxed factor...

THE ER.

DRINKING GAME

⚠ **THE WORLD'S FAVOURITE HOSPITAL DRAMA, GETS THE BEER-SOAKED DRINKING GAME TREATMENT.**

ESSENTIAL SUPPLIES
Lots of ER episodes on video. Beer.

A popular game for devotees of the show, **The ER Drinking Game** operates on similar rules to other themed games – if any of the actions below occur onscreen, you must pay the drinking penalty specified. So, simply pick a character, settle down with a tape of the show, crack open a couple of cans and prepare for action. Take a drink if any of your characters do any of the actions listed here: (note: this game covers all episodes of **ER**, but is particularly playable with the earlier shows).

If you picked Dr. Greene, take a drink every time that:
- He cheats on wife (early episodes only).
- He goes out with someone from the ER.
- He doesn't wear his green ER scrubs.
- He tries to leave the ER at the end of the shift, but is held up by a new emergency that he just HAS to deal with.
- He manages to say "goodnight" and leaves the ER.
- He encourages or gives some advice to a fellow worker.
- He forgets an important appointment because he is too busy saving lives in the ER.
- He goes against one of Dr. Weaver's "recommendations".

If you picked Dr. Carter, take a drink every time that:

• He acts like Dr. Benton.

• He flirts with a female member of staff.

• We see Dr. Carter's grandmother.

• He says something sarcastic about Benton.

• He learns a new procedure or technique.

• He saves a patient (drink triple if he loses a patient).

• He has an encounter with a medical student.

• He is the victim of a practical joke.

• He acts cooler than he actually is.

• He calls for a consult.

If you picked Dr. Ross, take a drink every time that:

• He stares at Hathaway across a crowded ER.

• He tries to see Hathaway off duty at an inappropriate time and gets rejected (if your watching the new series, change this to 'each time he kisses Hathaway').

• A patient reminds Dr. Ross of the importance of true love.

• He sleeps with Hathaway.

• He calls social services in to help with a patient.

• He says the word "kiddo".   (continued overleaf)

- He ruffles any child's hair.
- He does something to jeopardize his career.
- He does something to save his career.
- His dad contacts him. He sees his dad.
- He can't keep a secret told to him in the strictest confidence.

If you picked Dr. Benton, take a drink every time that:
- He clashes with other medical staff.
- He allows Carter do to a new procedure.
- He gets something wrong during a routine operation.
- He says something sarcastic.
- He goes on a date.
- Apologizes to another member of staff for his arrogance.
- He muscles in on someone else's procedure.
- Says something kind to any ER member.
- Seems to actually care about a patient.

If you picked Nurse Hathaway, take a drink every time that:
- She looks at Dr Ross across a crowded ER.
- She is not wearing her usual pink scrubs.
- She goes out of her way to help a patient.
- She mentions the word 'clinic'.
- She quits.
- She goes out on a date with somebody other than Dr. Ross.

If you picked Jeannie, take a drink every time that:
- Any nurse tells her, "That's a P.A. Job".
- She tells any nurse, "That's a nurse's job".
- She mentions that she is married.
- Her ex-husband appears or is mentioned in a conversation.
- She talks to anyone about being HIV positive.

- She gets worried when she attempts an internal procedure.
- She gets fired.
- She sleeps with Dr. Benton.
- She sleeps with anybody else from the ER.

If you picked Dr. Weaver, take a drink every time that:
- Somebody knocks her cane away.
- She contradicts another doctor, quotes the regulations or mentions budgetary restraints.
- Someone makes fun of her.
- She has an argument with another doctor or a patient's family.
- She makes a "recommendation" to Dr. Greene.
- She goes out on a date with somebody.
- She complains.

If you picked Jerry, take a drink every time that:
- He appears on screen in a wildly-coloured shirt.
- He corrects someone that he is the "emergency services coordinator"
- He appears in a costume of some sort.
- He is involved with something decidedly dodgy.
- He blows up an ambulance with a rocket launcher (quite specific this one, so drink your whole pint).

If you picked Dr. Lewis, take a drink every time that:
- She gets in an argument with another doctor.
- She goes out on a date.
- Chloe appears.
- Chloe runs away.
- Chloe's boyfriend appears.
- Chloe reappears, with a new boyfriend.
- Chloe claims she'll take care of "Little Susie".

(continued overleaf)

- Chloe smokes/drinks while talking about her baby.
- She kisses another ER doctor.
- Someone calls her "Big Susie".
- She brings "Little Susie" into the ER.
- She has Ross examine "Little Susie".
- She gets somebody in the ER to watch "Little Susie".

If you picked Dr. Del Amico, take a drink every time that:
- She and Dr. Carter seem to get close.
- She rejects Dr. Carter.
- She loses a patient.
- She complains about the size of her apartment.
- She flicks back her hair.
- She mentions her boyfriend (drink double if you actually get to see him).

If you picked Dr. Cordet, take a drink every time that:
- She flirts with Dr. Benton.
- She flirts with another member of the ER staff.
- She performs a new procedure.
- Someone mentions the fact that she's British.
- She mentions England, the NHS or her home.
- She kisses Dr. Benton.
- Someone calls her 'Lizzie'.

Bonus drinking. Take a drink every time that:
- Someone orders O- Neg in the ER.
- Someone orders a portable chest or a chest X-ray.
- Someone orders a Chem-7.
- Someone shouts 'Stat!'.
- Someone calls Dr. Carter something other than "Carter".

- A fireman in full firefighting gear (plus a blackened face) appears.
- Anyone mentions how little sleep they get.
- A policeman appears.
- Someone shows up in the ER having been dragged away from a grand ball, dinner engagement, day off, etc.
- The ER crew watch the scene of an accident on TV.
- A patient arrives at the ER by air ambulance.
- A member of the ER staff comes in on a gurney.
- Someone treats a young pregnant girl who can't tell her parents about the baby.
- Someone treats a patient who is really just after more drugs to feed his/her addiction.
- An old person is admitted, but he/she wants to be left alone to die.
- Someone sleeps in the ER.
- A gang member comes in as a patient.
- Someone pulls out a gun in the ER.
- Someone uses the lift.

Bolloxed factor...

S-M-A-S-H

 A SIMPLE DRINKING GAME THAT QUICKLY TURNS MASH INTO SMASHED.

ESSENTIAL SUPPLIES
Episodes of the old Korean War comedy, MASH. Beer.

It's so simple, it's a wonder that most of us didn't think of this effective game before. Just pop on a couple of episodes of **MASH**, watch them back-to-back and take a drink whenever anybody mentions somebody's rank – i.e. **Corporal**, **Major**, **Private**, etc. You can add to this by drinking whenever anybody says **'doctor'**, but if you do, we don't expect the game to last very long.

 Hints & Tips
Added authenticity for this game (like James Bond) means drinking martinis, but they must be "as dry as a dustbowl".

Bolloxed factor...

THE ORIGINAL STAR TREK

DRINKING GAME

⚠ **BOLDLY GO WHERE NO MEN HAVE GONE BEFORE WITH THE STARSHIP ENTERPRISE AND A CRATE OF BEER.**

ESSENTIAL SUPPLIES
Episodes of the original, Kirk-starring Star Trek. Beer.

Please note: This is NOT **The Next Generation Drinking Game**. This entertainment is based upon the original **Star Trek** – the **Star Trek** with Kirk, Bones and Spock; the Star Trek where the engines **"cannae take it, Captain"**; the **Star Trek** where the guys in the red jumpers have a life expectancy of about ten minutes if they're chosen to accompany Kirk on a planetary mission. So, watch closely and take a sip from your drink if anything listed below happens onscreen:

- Kirk gets the girl.
- Kirk gets the alien girl.
- Kirk outwits a super computer.
- Kirk worries about violating the Prime Directive. Then violates it anyway.
- Kirk's shirt gets ripped in a fight.
- Kirk takes responsibility for the whole crew.
- Kirk says "Phasers on stun".

- Spock shows faint signs of emotion.

(continued overleaf)

215

- Spock uses the Vulcan neck pinch.
- Spock gazes into his science computer and sees more than just a blue light.
- Spock says "Illogical".
- Spock says "Fascinating".
- Spock says "Indeed".

- Bones says "He's dead, Jim."
- Bones points out that "I'm a doctor, not a [insert job description here]". I.e. a mechanic, gardener, etc.
- Scotty complains about the state of the warp engines and the speed requested by the captain.

- Against all the odds, Scotty pulls off a technological feat that's never been done before. Usually with a cotton bud, some wire and a roll of sticky-back plastic.
- Chekov promotes Russian history.
- Chekov says "But Keptin...."

- Sulu sets course or Sulu has the con.

- Uhura says "Hailing frequencies open".
- Uhura opens a channel in all frequencies and all languages.

- A security guard in a red shirt dies on an alien planet.
- The away team's weapons are powerless against a new alien.
- The transporter system is inoperative.
- Dilithium crystals are drained, broken or missing.
- The shields are about to collapse.
- A newly discovered planet is "much like Earth".

Bolloxed factor...

CHEERS!

THE STAR TREK: TNG DRINKING GAME

BOLDLY GO WITH THE NEW ENTERPRISE (AND A NEW SET OF CLICHES), WHERE NO MAN HAS GONE BEFORE.

ESSENTIAL SUPPLIES
Episodes of Star Trek: The Next Generation on video. Beer.

There are two ways to play **The Star Trek: TNG Game**. The first is to drink whenever certain actions/events occur in an episode (we've called this **TNG 1**). The second is to drink whenever the characters in the show say specific lines of dialogue or perform specific actions (we've called this version, **TNG 2**). Whichever one you elect to play, the rules are simple to follow: check the lists below and if any of the actions/dialogue appears in the episode you are watching, take a sip from your drink. Note: if the game isn't working fast enough for you, up the penalty to two sips, then three and so on. But prepare yourself, this list is a big one...

TNG 1 – take a drink (or two) whenever...
- A crewmember straightens his/her uniform.
- A crewmember drinks in 10-Forward.
- A crewmember is seen in casual clothes.
- A crewmember is seen in dress uniform.
- A minor, unnamed crewmember gets a token line of dialogue.
- A character is referred to by their first name. I.e. Jean Luc, Deanna, etc.
- Transporter Room 3 is used.

- A shuttlecraft is used.
- Someone reads a book.
- Someone mentions the state of the ship's Dilithium crystals.
- Someone adopts a persona in a Holodeck program.
- Someone receives a cure-all shot of drugs from Dr. Crusher.
- A new alien is a thinly-disguised human with a differently shaped head.
- The Prime Directive is mentioned.
- The Prime Directive is broken.
- An alien intelligence mentions "humanity's potential" or how "mankind stands out in the universe".
- An "Old Earth Saying" is mentioned.
- The holodeck appears in its "natural" state. I.e. black walls with orange/yellow squares.
- The Enterprise is hurled somewhere by an alien force we will never understand, to participate in some sort of intergalactic test.
- Klingon is spoken. Somebody says K'plah.
- The ship's computer calmly informs the crew that the shields are weakening and that there's a hull breach.
- Picard or Riker order a course change by quoting the exact X, Y, and Z coordinates.
- A new alien ship is revealed.
- The sensors won't work due to generic "interference".
- The communicators don't work.

(continued overleaf)

- The transporter is unable to lock onto the away team on the surface.
- There's a yellow Alert.
- There's a Red Alert.
- There's an Intruder Alert.
- Another Captain or Starfleet officer is shown.
- There is a countdown.
- Someone stops the countdown.
- Bridge command is handed over to another member of the crew.
- A log entry is made by Picard.
- A log entry is made by someone other than Picard.
- A stardate is mentioned.
- An Old Earth Date is mentioned.
- Someone requests that an image on the main viewer be magnified.
- The ship/crew is seconds away from disaster.
- The transporter room beams someone aboard seconds after their ship explodes.
- Someone quotes Shakespeare.
- There's a fight.
- The Enterprise is taken over by an alien intelligence.
- Everybody's weapons are useless against a new alien intelligence.
- Phaser power is transferred to the shields.
- Someone fiddles around with the shield harmonics.
- A shuttlecraft is launched.
- A probe is launched.
- Someone mentions Jack Crusher.
- Someone is seen out of uniform.
- The Enterprise is boarded by hostiles.
- The auto-destruct sequence is activated.
- A principle character is put on trial.
- The Enterprise is captured in a nebula or large gas cloud that messes with the ships navigational array, its sensors and its weapons,

rendering the crew 'helpless and blind'.
- The Enterprise encounters an unknown energy form.

TNG 2 – take a drink (or two) whenever...
- Somebody says: "Open hailing frequencies".
- Somebody says: "Medical emergency".
- Somebody says: "Belay that order".
- Somebody says: "Energize".
- Somebody says: "Hell", "Damn" and other swearing.
- Somebody says: "It's not like anything I've ever seen before"
- Somebody says: "Impossible"
- Somebody says: "Shut up, Wesley"
- Somebody says: "On screen"
- Somebody says: "Understood"
- Somebody says: "Set phasers on..."
- Somebody says: "Acknowledged"
- Somebody says: "Priority One"
- Somebody says: "Just a little more time...!"

- Picard says: "Make it so"
- Picard says: "Engage"
- Picard says: "Come"
- Picard says: "Captain's Log"
- Picard says: "Captain's Log, Supplemental"
- Picard says: "Proceed"
- Picard says: "Number One"
- Picard straightens his uniform.
- Picard drinks tea.
- Picard requests a Level One Diagnostic.
- Picard makes a speech that saves the day and means they don't have to fight.

- Picard leaves the ship to lead an away team.
- Picard demonstrates knowledge of a foreign language.
- Picard feels uncomfortable around women and children.
- Picard quotes Shakespeare.
- Picard leaves the bridge during a crisis to talk with another character. I.e. Guinan.
- Picard reveals some personal feelings to Dr. Crusher.
- Picard takes a message from Starfleet in his ready room.
- Picard takes the helm.
- Picard calls a meeting.

- Worf says: "Impressive".
- Worf says: "Admirable".
- Worf says: "Grrrrr".
- Worf says: "I am a Klingon".
- Worf says: "Klingons do not..."
- Worf says: "Security Override!"
- Worf wins a fight.
- Worf throws someone in the brig.
- Worf asks for a human custom to be explained.
- Worf makes a suggestion that is ignored.
- Worf makes a reference to his sexual prowess.
- Worf participates in a bizarre Klingon ritual.

- Data says: "Fascinating".
- Data says: "Accessing".
- Data says: "Intriguing".
- Data says: "I am an android".
- Data says: "I cannot feel emotions".
- Data uses his superhuman android strength.
- Data uses his superior android speed.
- Someone peels back Data's hair and plugs him into a computer.
- Data gets cut off mid-sentence.
- Data is cut off while spouting a list of synonyms.
- Data asks another character to explain "An Old Earth Saying".
- Data analyses and manages to use alien technology within five minutes of seeing it.
- Data tries to be human.
- Data gives an approximate value of something to several decimal places.
- Data twitches his head.
- Data gets kissed by another character. His eyes remain open. He looks confused.
- Data is told by another character that he has done well and that he's more human than he thinks.
- Data is used to save the ship, or in a situation that is too dangerous for humans.

- Riker says: "Hell."
- Riker says: "What the hell is going on?"
- Riker says: "With pleasure, sir"
- Riker straightens his uniform.
- Riker thrusts his chin out with a smug look.
- Riker acts blatantly like a young, bearded Kirk.
- Riker gets the girl.

(continued overleaf)

- Riker spends an episode with an annoying smirk on his face.

- LaForge says: "I lost a lot of good people down there".
- LaForge says: "Maybe not" in response to a seemingly impossible situation that looks like the Enterprise will be destroyed.
- LaForge says: "I'm workin' on it!"
- LaForge gets his visor knocked off.
- LaForge adjusts the power to the warp engines, fiddles with the shield harmonics, diverts power from A to B, etc.
- LaForge removes his visor.

- Dr Crusher says: "This won't hurt a bit."
- Dr Crusher says: "This shouldn't be happening."
- Dr Crusher says: "Nothing yet, but we're working on it."
- Dr Crusher says: "He's dead."
- Dr Crusher says: "He's gone..."
- Dr Crusher says: "This man is dying!"
- Dr Crusher can't figure out a medical problem, or cure a disease until the last five minutes of the episode.
- Dr Crusher orders injured crewmembers/aliens to be beamed "directly to sickbay".
- Dr Crusher appears on the bridge.
- Dr Crusher appears in her lab coat.
- Dr Crusher explains a simple cut as an 'abrasion'.
- Dr Crusher performs major surgery.
- Dr Crusher shows maternal instinct.
- Dr Crusher loses, despite her best efforts, a patient in sickbay.

- Troi says: "What do you think about that?"
- Troi says "Are you troubled?"
- Troi says "Mother! Please...!"

- Troi senses something dangerous or deadly.
- Troi mentions Betazed or that she is a Betazoid.
- Troi cries.
- Troi is chatted up.
- Troi rolls her eyes.

- Wesley says: "It's easy!"
- Wesley says: "Wow!", "Gee!", "Ooh!"
- Wesley inexplicably saves the day through a combination of luck and rudimentary Starfleet training.
- Wesley inexplicably saves the day and nobody thanks him.
- Wesley can't shake off his Riker-esque annoying grin.
- Wesley works on a new science project.
- Wesley protests that he's not just "some kid anymore".

Bolloxed factor...

🍾🍾🍾🍾🍾

THE STAR TREK: DS9

DRINKING GAME

⚠ ALL THE BEER-BASED FUN OF THE STAR TREK UNIVERSE, BUT ON A SPACE STATION.

ESSENTIAL SUPPLIES
Far too many episodes of DS9 for comfort. Beer.

A gain, another simple TV-based game. Just pick a character that appears in **DS9** (i.e. Sisko, Quark, Odo, Dax, Bashir, etc.) and take a drink every time that your character either **(a)** has a confrontation with another character, or **(b)** has a fight with another character. With emotional problems, terrorism and petty conflicts rife on the Star Trek station, these two rules should keep your drinking hand more than busy. But if you require even more excuses to lift your beer in an SF salute, then why not **drink** whenever any of the following events appear onscreen...

• Something isn't working properly on the space station.
• A character says 'DS9'.
• A fight breaks out on the promenade and Odo is called to break it up.
• The space station or the Defiant are viewed from outside.
• The cog airlocks are shown opening or closing.
• Any other door is shown opening.
• Somebody mentions Bejor with fondness.
• Somebody mentions Bejor with malice.

- Sisko threatens somebody.
- Someone tries to chat up Dax.
- Odo acts like Spock and Data and is puzzled by a facet of human behaviour.
- Dr. Bashir has a plan. But it's rubbish.

And take TWO drinks every time that:

- Someone is shown using the elevator in the control room.
- A shuttlecraft is shown.
- Odo shapeshifts.
- Quark or another Ferengi mention 'The Rules Of Acquisition'.
- O'Brien uses the transporters.
- Jake Sisko gets in trouble.
- Kira has a case of divided loyalties.

And take THREE drinks every time that:

- A character from Star Trek: TNG makes an appearance.
- Sisko backs down from a fight.
- Odo does something intentionally humorous.
- Dr. Bashir does something clever.
- O'Brien is jury-rigs something to save the station from disaster.
- Quark does something selfless

Bolloxed factor...

227

THE STAR TREK: VOYAGER DRINKING GAME

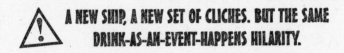

A NEW SHIP, A NEW SET OF CLICHES. BUT THE SAME DRINK-AS-AN-EVENT-HAPPENS HILARITY.

ESSENTIAL SUPPLIES
Episodes of Star Trek Voyager. Beer.

Pop an episode of **Star Trek**'s newest series into your VCR and knock back some of your favourite alcoholic beverage every time that the following actions/events occur. It's the same **Star Trek** formula, but a whole new set of drinking reasons. So, get your booze ready and take ONE sip whenever...

- Janeway adjusts her hair during a moment of disaster or extreme danger.
- Janeway drinks coffee.
- The ship's Holographic doctor reminds a crewmember to turn him off.
- The ship's Holographic doctor is unsympathetic.
- The ship's Holographic doctor makes a smart remark.
- Tuvok uses the phrase "there must be a logical explanation."
- Chakotay loses himself in an old Indian ritual or something important to his 'tribe'.
- Chakotay has a flashback or a vision.
- Chakotay mentions his ancestors.
- Neelix serves up some new food and nobody eats it.

- Somebody complains about Neelix's cooking.
- Somebody mentions Kess's lifespan.
- Neelix offers to help with a situation he plainly knows nothing about.
- Neelix gets jealous of Tom Paris.
- The crew discover a new race that have warp engines.
- The crew discover a new race that have better warp engines, weapons and systems than they do.
- An alien is discovered who is basically humanoid, but with a differently-shaped/latex-enhanced head.
- Somebody mentions that they need to stop for repairs or spare parts.
- Somebody enters the Holodeck.
- Somebody enters Paris' Holodeck bar program.
- Torres figures out a new way to avoid a 'warp core breach'.

And take TWO sips whenever...

- The holographic doctor leaves sickbay.
- A new alien that doesn't communicate through the translators.
- A new particle is mentioned.
- Kess uses her psychic abilities.
- Neelix's help is useful.
- The crew mention "home", "DS9" or any other major (continued overleaf)

character from the Star Trek universe.
- Someone likes some of Neelix's food
- Tuvok performs a 'mind meld' or a 'vulcan neck pinch'.

And take THREE sips whenever...

- The crew pass up a chance to go home to save one of their number.
- Somebody dies.

Bolloxed factor...

CHEERS!

THE WITHNAIL AND I DRINKING GAME

⚠ **THE SIMPLE INSTRUCTIONS THAT FOLLOW ULTIMATELY LEAD TO A DEADLY DRINKING GAME.**

ESSENTIAL SUPPLIES
Withnail And I on video. A wide variety of booze.

Simple rules, simple game, simpley pissed.

(1) Start watching **Withnail And I** on video.

(2) Note down exactly what drinks the two lead characters consume during the movie.

(3) Pop down to your local Off License and buy the types and the amounts of drink that you have recently noted down.

(4) Watch **Withnail And I** again.

(5) Drink exactly what the characters drink, when they drink them, and in the same quantities.

Hints & Tips
It's best to save up for this a while, it's going to set you back a lot of money to try and keep up with these two jokers.

Bolloxed factor...

THE RAIDERS OF THE LOST ARK

DRINKING GAME

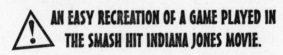

⚠ **AN EASY RECREATION OF A GAME PLAYED IN THE SMASH HIT INDIANA JONES MOVIE.**

ESSENTIAL SUPPLIES
Several bottles of harsh vodka. 10 shot glasses.

Remember the scene in **Raiders Of The Lost Ark**? Picture the feisty Ms. Marian Ravenwood – she's the eventual heroine, the one who owns the bar in Russia and wears the vital headpiece to the Staff Of Ra around her neck.

Before Indiana Jones arrives, before the Herr Flick-type Nazi (with his coathanger) and his goons tear up the establishment looking for the ancient artifact, Ms. Ravenwood competes in a **drinking game** with one of her more surly patrons.

It works like this: she stands 10 shot glasses in two rows, one row of five glasses for each person. These glasses are then filled to the brim with the deadliest vodka she can find – this stuff can take paint of walls, it's a couple of degrees away from being an efficient jet fuel, etc. Once full, the two drinking combatants simply drink one glass in turn, repeating the filling-up process until somebody falls on the floor in a

drunken stupor. All you have to do is recreate this drinking experience, with shot glasses of your own and the meanest vodka you can find in the nearest Off Licence. **Two people enter** the game, but only one may leave slightly sober...

Bolloxed factor...

CHEERS!

THE KING OF THE HILL

DRINKING GAME

⚠️ **ANOTHER CARTOON, MERCILESSLY ADAPTED FOR BEER-DRINKING PURPOSES. IT'S SHAMEFUL...**

ESSENTIAL SUPPLIES
Episodes of King Of The Hill on video. Beer.

The usual rules apply – start watching **King Of The Hill**, have cans/glasses of beer at the ready, and simply start drinking whenever any of the following actions/events occurs onscreen:

- Boomhower mumbles (1 finger/sip)
- Luane cries (1 finger/sip)
- Anyone drinks beer (1 finger/sip)
- We see the Indian (1 finger/sip)
- Peggy Hill gives her insight into a problem (1 finger/sip)
- A racist comment is made (1 finger/sip)
- Luane talks about or attends Beauty School (1 finger/sip)
- Dale expresses his paranoia (2 fingers/sips)
- Bill talks about his ex-wife (2 fingers/sips)
- Bobby panics (2 fingers/sips)
- Someone gets married (3 fingers/sips)

Bolloxed factor...

THE FRASIER
DRINKING GAME

⚠ **WHAT WOULD THE TV SHRINK READ INTO THE FACT THAT HIS LIFE IS NOW A DRINKING GAME?**

ESSENTIAL SUPPLIES
Several epsiodes of Frasier. Beer.

ypcially, start watching an episode of **Frasier**, raise your glass and swig some booze back whenever you see any of the following happen during the show.

For starters, take **one drink** whenever:

• Frasier says: "I'm listening."

• Frasier takes a swipe at the seedy, fly-by-night nature of Roz's love life.

• Niles takes a swipe at the seedy, fly-by-night nature of Roz's love life.

• Frasier mentions anything that's vaguely related to his previous TV show, **Cheers**. This can include: the bar itself, Boston, any of the characters he used to know (Sam, Diane, Norm, Cliff, Carla, etc.) **Drink double** if he mentions Lilith or his son Frederick. **Drink triple** if either of them turn up in the show. **Drink four times** the usual swig if he mentions Diane Chambers; **five times** the norm if she turns up in the show.

• Frasier threatens the dog.

• Niles makes a snide comment about Frasier's fast-receding hairline.

• Niles makes a snide comment about Frasier's love-life. Or lack of it.

• Niles dusts his chair.

• Daphne mentions any of her brothers or Granny Moon.

• Daphne makes an unintended but highly suggestive (continued overleaf)

comment that causes the poor, lustful Niles to react in a leering, over-the-top way.
- Roz mentions a 'hot date' she had the other night.
- Roz whinges about NOT having a 'hot date' last night.
- Bulldog makes a sexist comment.

Drink twice the normal dosage whenever:
- Frasier's first wife turns up.
- Frasier's agent Bibi appears.
- You manage to guess who the celebrity caller is on the phone-in show.
- Frasier wears shorts.
- Niles and Frasier are shown as kids.

Bolloxed factor...

THE FRIENDS
DRINKING GAME

⚠️ **SO MANY CHARACTERS, SO MANY SITUATIONS...
YOUR CHANCES OF STAYING SOBER ARE NOT GOOD.**

ESSENTIAL SUPPLIES
A stack of Friends videos. Beer.

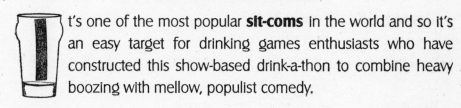 t's one of the most popular **sit-coms** in the world and so it's an easy target for drinking games enthusiasts who have constructed this show-based drink-a-thon to combine heavy boozing with mellow, populist comedy.

And without further ado, here's how the game works. Just settle down in front of the TV, rip open that crate of lager, pop open a bottle and take **a gulp** whenever any of the actions listed below occur on the TV screen. So watch to see whether:

• Phoebe says "duh!"
• Chandler waves his arms around in a wild manner while trying to say something important.
• Ross takes longer to say a sentence than a normal person would.
• Rachel calls someone "Honey".
• A celebrity guest makes an appearance.
• Any of the six characters drink or mention coffee.
• The exterior of Central Park is shown.
• The exterior of Monica/Rachel's and Chandler/Joey's apartment building is shown.
• Any of the six are shown at their places of work.
• Any of the main character's parents show up.

(continued overleaf)

- Any two or more main characters hug.
- Joey doesn't understand something that is obvious to everybody else.
- The hallway between Monica/Rachel's and Chandler/Joey's apartment is shown.
- Gunther shows just how much he loves Rachel.
- An animal is shown (Marcel the monkey, the duck, etc.)
- Ross and Rachel argue.

Now it starts to get interesting. Take two gulps if any of the following take place:

- Phoebe plays a song on her guitar (add an extra gulp if it's Smelly Cat).
- The inside of Phoebe's apartment is shown.
- The inside of Ross' apartment is shown.
- All six main characters hang out in Monica/Rachel's apartment.
- Anyone makes a reference to an old TV show.
- Joey goes on a film/TV/theatre audition.
- Ross mentions Ben, Carol, or Susan.
- Any of the six main characters kiss a non-main character.
- Ross gets jealous.
- Phoebe drives her grandma's taxi.
- Monica tidies up.
- Joey and Chandler buy a new piece of furniture.
- Joey and Chandler build a new piece of furniture.
- All six main characters play a game.

But to make it really exciting... drink triple the usual gulp if any of the stuff below happens:

- Joey actually understands the opposite sex.

238

- Marcel returns.
- Phoebe says something sensible.
- Monica dates a relatively normal person her own age. At least twice.
- Ben has a major speaking part in any episode.
- Phoebe's dad arrives.
- Dr. Green is nice to Ross.
- Janice laughs.
- Janice says "Oh. My. God.."
- Chandler drops his sarcastic, cynical facade.

Bolloxed factor...

CHEERS!

THE PRINCESS BRIDE

DRINKING GAME

 **ONE OF THE GREATEST FILMS EVER (WHAT DO YOU MEAN YOU'VE NEVER SEE IT) GETS THE BOOZED-UP TREATMENT.**

ESSENTIAL SUPPLIES
A copy of the fabulous (and often overlooked) Princess Bride. Beer.

f you haven't seen this classic fantasy comedy then rush out to your local video store and do so now. Why? Because you can't hope to play **The Princess Bride** Drinking Game if you're not anally familiar with the plot and its characters. For the rest of you, who've already discovered the delights of this truly excellent movie, crack open a beer, settle back and drink back those beers whenever any of the following actions or events occur:

- Fred Savage's character whines like a spoilt, impatient brat.
- Buttercup describes Wesley as a 'farm boy'.
- Wesley says: "As you wish."
- Someone explains about the wonders of true love, how it doesn't come along very often, how it transcends space and time... you know the sort of thing.
- Someone mentions the name 'Humperdink'.
- Vessini says: "inconceivable!"
- There is a sword fight.
- Inigo Montoya says: "My name is Inigo Montoya, you killed my father,

prepare to die."

- Bishop Peter Cook says his r's wrong. Drink once for each cock-eyed pronunciation.
- Humperdink talks about or uses his tracking skills.
- The King speaks.
- Fezzik speaks.
- Wesley insults Humperdink.

Bolloxed factor...

CHEERS!

THE SOUTH PARK DRINKING GAME

⚠️ **A GAME WHERE THE WORDS "OH MY GOD, THEY KILLED KENNY!" CAN GET YOU INTO BIG TROUBLE.**

ESSENTIAL SUPPLIES
A collection of South Park episodes. Beer.

nother adult 'toon, another set of simple rules to turn it into a drinking game. Line up a couple of episodes of **South Park**, get some mates round, set up the beers and drink down the booze whenever any of the following actions or events occur:

- Kenny dies.
- Rats carry off Kenny's head.
- Cartman says: "Son of a bitch!"
- An animal is used in any sexual manner.
- Someone farts.
- Someone farts and it's on fire (drink twice).
- Chef sings.
- Chef makes up a nonsensical word.
- Mr. Hat swears.
- Kyle kicks the baby.
- The baby says: "Don't kick the baby."
- Someone says: "Sweet!"
- Cartman says he's not fat, just big-boned.

- Mr. Garrison explains his debased version of history.
- Kenny speaks.
- Jesus appears.
- Any Jewish reference is made.
- Kyle's mom is called a bitch.
- Anything explodes.
- Cartman is called a fatass.
- There is a non-fart-related reference to arses.
- The cows appear.
- Kyle says: "...make sweet love...."
- Cartman says: "Kick ass!"
- Stan gets the crap beat out of him by his sister.
- Chef mentions love.
- Cartman says: "Beefcake!"
- The bus driver yells.
- Special guests appear.
- Chef swears.
- Chef refers to the boys as crackers.

(continued overleaf)

- Officer Barbrady tries to cover up an incident.
- Stan knows the moral of the story.
- Cartman mentions pie.
- The kids look at Terence and Phillip farting on each other.
- The genetic engineer wants to reform his mad scientist ways.
- The genetic engineer uses "lusciously" when he speaks.
- Ned sings with his cancer kazoo.
- Real pictures are used as posters in the background.
- Someone other than Kenny dies.

Bolloxed factor...

THE RESERVOIR DOGS

DRINKING GAME

⚠️ **DRUNKS TO THE LEFT OF ME, DRUNKS TO THE RIGHT, HERE I AM, PISSED IN THE MIDDLE WITH YOU...**

ESSENTIAL SUPPLIES
One video of Reservoir Dogs. Beer.

An easy game, with the easiest rules you'll ever come across. The key to drinking in **The Reservoir Dogs Drinking Game** is NOT to quaff, scull, imbibe and down whenever an action occurs on the screen (i.e. the botched heist, the ear-slicing scene, etc.), but simply to take a drink whenever any of the characters in the movie uses the word **'f*ck'**. Our congratulations to any of you that manage to keep to this one-swig-per-f*ck rule and make to the end of the movie with your sanity (and the majority of your brain cells) intact. If you don't, we won't think any less of you. Put it this way... have you any idea how many times the F-word is used in **Reservoir Dogs**? It's more than you think...

 Hints & Tips
You can, we're sure, think of other movies where the same game can be played. None are as good as this one...

Bolloxed factor...

BAT BEER

⚠ AFTER BAT-BELTS, BAT-A-RANGS, BATMOBILES, BATBOATS
AND BAT-BOMBS, YOU WON'T BE ABLE TO STAND.

ESSENTIAL SUPPLIES
Any Batman movie or episodes of the old 60's TV series. Lots of beer.

A nother oh-so-simple game that makes watching the lesser Bat-movies much more pleasurable. In fact, it's a game that has all the simplicity of **SMASH** and **The Reservoir Dogs Drinking Game**, an entertainment built around such a basic idea, it's amazing that nobody has come across it before. What is it? It is simply this: whenever anyone in any of the movies or the TV shows mentions the word **'Bat'**, you have to take a drink. That means after every Batman, Batmobile, Bat-a-rang, Bat signal, Batgirl, Bat-radar, and so on. And like the **SMASH** game, the simplicity of the rules hide a game that sticks you on the fast-track to alcoholic oblivion.

 Hints & Tips
Similar amusement can be enjoyed with certain films and the word 'super', or cartoons and 'spider'. You get the plan.

Bolloxed factor...

BUILD YOUR OWN TV

DRINKING GAME

⚠ **IF ONE OF YOUR FAVOURITE SHOWS ISN'T LISTED HERE, WHY NOT MAKE UP YOUR OWN DRINK-A-THON?**

ESSENTIAL SUPPLIES
Your favourite TV show. Some paper. A pen. Beer.

As you've probably noticed, most TV and movie-based drinking games require their subject to have a **large** number of regularly repeated features or cliches. If you can find these in a TV show then making up a drinking game should be as easy as making a list.

For example, you might want to have a crack at writing down an **EastEnders Drinking Game** – drink whenever Bianca shouts "Ricky"; drink when Frank laughs; drink when Phil or Grant threaten another person in the square; drink whenever somebody orders a pint in the Queen Vic; drink whenever anybody sits down in the Park; the list can go on and on. Basically, all you have to look for in a programme is the pattern. Once you've found this, you can easily build an effective drinking game around it.

So here's a few pointers – **(1)** Look at the drinking games on these pages and learn what makes them tick, whether they are built around actions, events, quotes or something else. **(2)** Look at each of the

247

major characters in turn and isolate the catchphrases or gestures that they repeat from week to week. **(3)** A character might also do familiar tasks or visit the same locations in different episodes, this can be used to your advantage. **(4)** When you have a decent list of character actions and quotes, split them into three categories – Normal (for regular cliches); Rare (for cliches that may happen only a few times each episode) and Endangered Species (cliches that very, very rarely come along). Assign one, two and three sips/gulps/swigs to each category and you're ready to go...

Bolloxed factor...

MISCELLANEOUS SPORTS GAMES

⚠️ **A FEW SIMPLE WAYS TO LIVEN UP AN AFTERNOON'S SPORTING ACTION.**

ESSENTIAL SUPPLIES
Cricket. Football. Ten Pin Bowling. Tennis. Find a sport and simply add beer.

While there are many TV and movie-based drinking games, there are very few **games** that exist to liven up an afternoon's sport. Until now that is. Because here, we've attempted to gather together a collection of sports-based amusements that can liven up a football game, inject a little excitement into **Tennis** and allow you to drink while watching **Formula 1 Grand Prix racing**. So, digging into this jamboree bag of athleticism, we came up with...

The Football Drinking Game

This simple game allows you to drink and to enjoy a game of televised footy without having to constantly reference a list of actions and events. While it would be easy to construct a game that has you drinking whenever there's a pass, drinking double for a shot at goal, and drinking triple for a goal scored, you may find that the the rules below combine to make an enjoyable game that's heavy on the bladder but easy on the brain.

Here's how it works: played with two players, or with two equal teams, the **Football Drinking Game** is a test of drinking skill that is unlikely to last the full 90 minutes of a match. The basic idea is that each team must take a drink whenever the ball is in their side's half of the field, stopping when it passes over the half-way line to the

opposing side's half. By way of illustration, if Arsenal were playing Liverpool, one team would adopt Arsenal, the other Liverpool. Whenever the ball goes into the Arsenal half of the field, the Arsenal team drink from their beers; when the ball goes into Liverpool's half, the Liverpool team drink. The only extra rule is that the team members must drink **constantly** whenever the goalkeeper is holding the ball, stopping when he drops or kicks it. Enjoy...

The Formula 1 Drinking Game

There are many ways to take the fast-paced action of **F1** and turn it into a drinking game too. Each drinker could adopt one of the teams, taking a sip for each time one of the team's cars completes a lap. Or, more seasoned drinkers may like to try the **Pitstop variant**, where players only drink during pitstops in the race, but must keep drinking for the length of time the car on camera is stationary in the pitlane. Then there's the **Murray Walker** drinking game, where players take a sip every time that the voice of British Motor Racing makes a mistake or shouts **"Amazing"**, **"Look at that!!"** etc.

The Tennis Drinking Game

Is it just us, or is **Tennis** becoming an increasingly dull and unexciting game? Whatever your opinion, why not liven it up with **The Tennis Drinking Game**, an entertainment that seems to work best with the slowest type of tennis you can find – the Women's game. While Men's tennis is dominated by big- hitters and short rallies, Women's tennis is perfect for changing into a drinking game. Try these rules out for size: best played with two players, or with two teams, each side/player adopts one of the two tennis players. Then, whenever their tennis player hits the ball, they have to take a sip of beer (long rallies are a nightmare). Whenever the players sit down between games, is the only time that **Tennis Drinking Game** players are allowed to visit the toilet.

The Cricket Drinking Game

As a game of **cricket** can last all day, **The Cricket Drinking Game** is a solitary affair, best played by a single player who wants to get well-and-truly tanked on his/her own. The rules? One gulp per run of course. Or maybe, one drink (pint, half-pint or short) per man out. Or perhaps you could mutate a version of the word game **Buzz** – when a team's score reaches a multiples of, say, 3, 5 and 7 (or features any of those numbers in its score), then the players must drink a penalty. Try this if the prospect of one swig per run and a score of 250+ sounds a **wee bit** daunting.

The Golf Drinking Game

Either drink **one finger** of beer **per shot** played or (and it's my favourite) drink for the number of **seconds** a player's ball flies through the air. This is usually not very long and only happens two or three times a hole.

The Ten Pin Bowling Drinking Game

There are 10 pins standing at the bottom of the lane. A player comes up to bowl and knocks down 7 of the 10 with his/her first ball. Take the 7 downed pins away from the original 10 and that leaves 3. Therefore the other players must drink **3 fingers** of beer.

Bolloxed factor...

CHAPTER 7

PUB GAMES

Games with cards, dice, coins and other props are all very well, but if all you want is a game that requires no extras other than the pub you're sat in, this is the section for you. Admittedly, for some of these games you'll need some specialised equipment. But as most modern pubs are starting to carry pub games (like **Chess, Draughts, Kerplunk**, etc.) to keep their drinkers happy, finding the props mentioned in the games below shouldn't be too much of a problem. Of course, the clutter-free drinking games remain the most challenging and daring of all guzzling entertainments. How can you beat the dangerous simplicity of the **Pub Crawl**? How can you hope to equal the meshing of skill and drinking stamina tested by ye olde **Yard of Ale**? And how can you match the uncoordinated hilarity of what many people are starting to call **The Broom Handle** game? So pick a pub (or in the Crawl's case, several in close proximity) and settle down.

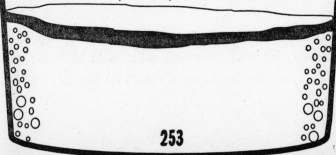

THE PUB CRAWL

⚠ A GAME AS OLD AS RECORDED TIME. WHICH IS PRETTY DAMNED OLD.

ESSENTIAL SUPPLIES
A large amount of pubs, in a very small area. Money.

ow come on. You know how this game works. You start off in a pub (let's call it the Fox And Hounds), drink one pint of lager (or a half-pint) and then move onto the next pub in the street (i.e. The Crown And Anchor) where you repeat the drinking ritual. Then you move onto the next pub (The Plough), the next. and so on until **(a)** you can't drink another drop, **(b)** the pubs shut or **(c)** you fall over and spend the night in the gutter next to a small cat nibbling at a three-day-old pork ball. It's a game enjoyed by thousands across the country, a game that works particularly well in towns with an obscene number of watering holes in close proximity to each other.

Variants:
The Three-Legged Pub Crawl. As in the traditional **Pub Crawl**, players move from pub to pub, drinking down an agreed measure of alcohol and moving on. **The Three-Legged Pub Crawl** gives the usual game a old playground twist. Simply stand two willing drunkards together, tie the right leg of one to the left leg of the other (creating 'three' legs) and set them out on the pub crawl as before. If you have trouble controlling your own legs after eight pints of Kronenbourg, imagine how tough it is to keep somebody else standing up...

Hints & Tips

Sensible people will make sure that everyone meets up beforehand and gets something decent to eat before piling on the booze.

The Fancy Dress Crawl. Again, see the Pub Crawl above but spice up the pub-wandering proceedings by dressing up in outlandish garb. How about an Army Captain, a priest, an Indian Brave or, by messing around with a cardboard box, a plunger, some small footballs (cut in half) and a dustbin lid, make your own Dr Who Dalek costume...

Monopoly Pub Crawl. Surely the ultimate pub crawl, the idea behind **Pub Monopoly** is to visit each street/station on the English Monopoly board (that's a grand total of 26) and to have a drink in each one. The only rule is that you have to complete the crawl in a single day, imbibing your liquids between the hours of 11am and 11pm. Obviously the best way to do this is to plan ahead, seeing which pubs along your route are open all day and which of them are only open at lunchtime and in the evening. We suggest having, perhaps, a half-pint in each pub. Force yourself to have a pint and you'll undoubtedly fail after 10+ stops. You might even land on the **Go To Jail** card...

The Circle Line Crawl. Similar to the **Monopoly Crawl**, this variant can only be played in London and involves riding around the famous Circle line, stopping at each station to **(a)** locate a pub and **(b)** drink beer. The game ends when every stop's been visited and a drink downed, or when you're pissed out of your face, stagger off the tube and get the last train to **Uxbridge**. This is especially humorous if you happen to live in **Chelsea**. (continued overleaf)

Pub Golf. Another Crawl innovation, **Pub Golf** takes the basic rules of the traditional **Pub Crawl** and forces a golfing theme onto it. Here's how it works: organise your players into pairs as if you were going to play the **Three-Legged Pub Crawl** variant. One player of the two will be the **'Professional'** player, which means that he/she will have to drink pints as the pair moves from pub to pub. The second player in the pair, will be known as the **'Amateur'** player, which in turn means that he/she will have to drink half-pints or shorts in every pub the pair visits. Like playing a round of golf, the teams must visit nine holes (pubs), each one of which has a Par 3 rating. What this means is that each player in the pair must down their drink in three gulps or less. The scores are combined so that if one player finishes his/her drink in 4 gulps, the other has only 2 gulps left (i.e. 3 + 3 = 6; 4 + 2 = 6) to finish his/her drink to get a par for the hole. However, if the pro player downs his/her drink in one go, this is considered a hole-in-one and both players can move onto the next hole. Shots are dropped going to the toilet (1 shot), spilling your drink (1 shot) or falling over (2 shots). The team with the highest overall score at the end of the nine-pub crawl loses the game and must drink a forfeit decided by the other participating players.

Bolloxed factor...

THE YARD OF ALE

⚠ **IT SEEMS EASY. A YARD OF ALE IS ONLY A COUPLE OF PINTS... IT'S HARDER THAN IT LOOKS.**

ESSENTIAL SUPPLIES
A pub with the traditional Yard O' Ale glass.

It's the simplest and probably the **most famous** pub game there is, but it's a vanishing art. Most pubs don't even serve ale, let alone have a traditional **yard glass**, but if you can find one, ask the barman to fill you up and then attempt to down the contents, in one, without spilling a drop. As mentioned above, this is trickier than it looks. At the beginning, the ale flows slowly and freely and gulping it down is just like drinking from a tall-necked glass. What you have to watch out for is the ale that's pooled in the **bulb** at the very end. When you get to a certain point, the pressure of the ale in the neck of the glass will have lessened (because you'll have drunk most of the beer), causing the beer in the bulb to shoot out unexpectedly and uncontrollably, **drenching** the drinker. The only way to avoid this is to twirl the long glass as you quaff, **turning the neck** slowly between your fingers until the contents have drained away. Whatever you do, don't try to do this twice in a row...

Hints & Tips
We prefer to drink our yards sitting down – it's what you'll be doing very shortly afterwards anyway, so plan ahead.

Bolloxed factor...

THE BROOM HANDLE GAME

 ANOTHER SIMPLE GAME WITH A SURPRISINGLY HIGH HUMOUR FACTOR.

ESSENTIAL SUPPLIES
A beer garden. Beer. A broom handle.

What else can you call it? It's **The Broom Handle** game. Simply, gather together a large group of friends and give everybody a pint of something strong and lager-like. The idea of the game is a simple one – one at a time the players drink **half** of their pint and run up the beer garden to a **broom handle** laying on the grass. The participating player then picks up the sweeping stick, puts the brush on the turf and holds the handle up vertically like a pole. Quickly, the player than place his forehead on the end of the vertically-standing broom handle and runs around it ten times. After the **tenth** rotation, all the player then has to do is run or walk back up the garden to drink the rest of his/her pint. Dizziness, however, should take control at this point, and the drunken player should hilariously **cartwheel** into the fence/flowerbed/tables, etc. The winner is the one who makes it back to their pint and drinks it. Losers get laughed at.

 ## Hints & Tips
Take a tip from ice figure-skaters and keep an eye on a fixed point as you twirl around. This is meant to help.

Bolloxed factor...

BOAT RACE

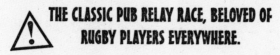

⚠ **THE CLASSIC PUB RELAY RACE, BELOVED OF RUGBY PLAYERS EVERYWHERE.**

ESSENTIAL SUPPLIES
Two teams. Beer. Clothes you don't mind getting wet.

Divide a group of wannabe drinkers into two equal teams. Give each member of the team a pint of the amber nectar and line them up in an organised row, one behind the other. The idea of the **Boat Race** is ludicrously simple – it's a trumped-up **relay** race, but with **beer**. When somebody shouts go (or drops a handkerchief, fires a gun, taps a table, whatever...) the team member at the head of the line starts drinking their pint as fast as they possibly can. When they've finished, they must quickly raise their empty glass and place it, upside down, on top of their head. This movement then signals the player behind to start draining the foamy contents their pint, and again when the player finishes, their glass must be placed upside down on top of their head. Play continues in this fashion until all of the players in the line have finished their drinks and have upturned pint glasses on their **heads**. The first team to finish all of their drinks and place all of their glasses in this position, wins the race. The losers then have to face a suitable drinking penalty...

Hints & Tips
Don't plan on moving on to any posh locations after playing this, you and your clothes will absolutely stink of beer.

Bolloxed factor...
🍾🍾🍾🍾🍾🍾🍾

JENGAHOLIC

 **A GAME THAT REQUIRES A HIGH DRINKING STAMINA AND STEADY HANDS.**

ESSENTIAL SUPPLIES
A box of Jenga blocks. Beer.

 ow that more pubs in the UK have games behind the bar, **Jengaholic** is just one of the many booze-related variants you can play. The idea is an easy one (although for this game, you're better off using your own **Jenga** set).

Before you build up your **Jenga** tower, painstakingly label each wooden block with some sort of action or drinking penalty, i.e. **'Take Off An Item Of Clothing"**, **"Drink Three Sips Of Beer"**, **"Tell A Player To Drink Three Sips"**, and so on. Then, quite obviously, when a player removes a block he/she must perform the action written on it. Failure to do so incurs a hefty drinking penalty, as does knocking the **Jenga** tower over. The primary rule is to drink and to keep drinking. Any other rules you make are purely to spice up the proceedings.

 Hints & Tips
Keep a bar towel on hand for wiping up any spillages. There's nothing worse than trying to play Jenga with wet fingers.

Bolloxed factor...

KER-DRUNK

⚠ **A PERVERSION OF THE CLASSIC KIDS GAME, NOW WITH MUCH HIGHER STAKES.**

ESSENTIAL SUPPLIES
A game of Kerplunk. A jug. Beer.

Like **Jengaholic**, **Ker-Drunk** is another game that takes a traditional gaming favourite and gives it a drink-related twist. It can be played in two ways.

Number 1: fill a jug with beer and play **Ker-Plunk** as usual. Whoever removes the plastic straw that makes all the marbles drop into the bottom, has to drink the contents of the jug.

Number 2 is slightly more deadly... Players take it in turns to pull out a straw from the **Ker-Plunk** tower. This time, however, every time a marble drops, the player responsible must add some of his drink (whatever that may be) to the empty jug. This process continues until a lethal **concoction** of drink froths in the jug and some unlucky soul pulls out the straw that makes the remaining marbles cascade into the bottom of the tower. When this happens, the unfortunate player must drink down the jug's contents. He/she may not want to play another game after doing so.

Hints & Tips
If you're playing version 2, be sure and choose drinks that don't mix well. Like Bailey's, Lager and white wine.

Bolloxed factor...

BEER CHESS

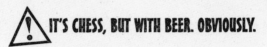 IT'S CHESS, BUT WITH BEER. OBVIOUSLY.

ESSENTIAL SUPPLIES
An oversized chessboard (failing this some bathroom tiles). Cans of beer.

As you'd expect, **Beer Chess** is played using beer as the pieces. And because the pieces are cans or bottles, you're going to require a slightly larger chessboard than usual. If you can't find one, a good alternative is to get a collection of white and black bathroom tiles. Laid out in a chessboard-style grid on the floor, they make a ideal playing surface for **Beer Chess** (for a more portable, pub-based board, try using different coloured beer coasters). As for the pieces, one player should play using bottles of beer, while the other should use cans.

A typical set-up might look something like this: White would play with – **8 pawns** = 8 bottle of Becks; **2 rooks** = 2 bottles of Heineken; **2 bishops** = 2 bottles of Miller Draught; **2 knights** = 2 bottles of Kronenbourg; **King** = bottle of Budweiser (the King of Beers, so the ads say); **Queen** = bottle of Grolsch. Black would then play with cans – 8 pawns = 8 cans of Carling Black Label; 2 rooks = 2 cans of Fosters; 2 bishops = 2 cans of Grolsch; 2 knights = 2 cans of Heineken; King = a can of Budweiser; Queen = a can of Special Brew. It might help to **label** the cans with a **black marker pen** so you don't forget which is which.

The rules for the game are as follows: **(1)** when a player moves a piece on the board, he/she must take a sip from the piece moved. **(2)** When a piece is captured by the opposing player, the owner of the captured piece must drink the contents of the can/bottle taken. **(3)** The

Hints & Tips

Never play this game with anyone you know to be from Russia. They can all play chess like Spassky and drink like Boris Yeltsin

'Castling' manoeuvre costs two sips from each piece to complete. **(4)** The Pawn move **'En Passant'** costs one sip. **(5)** If a pawn reaches the eighth rank on the board, the player can exchange it for a queen – the opposing player must drink the entire contents of the exchanged pawn. **(6)** Once a piece has been sipped, the piece MUST be moved. **(7)** When a player is put in **'check'**, the checked player must take a sip from the King piece. **(8)** When one player is checkmated, the losing player must drink the contents of his remaining pieces.

Bolloxed factor...

CHEERS!

BOOZE DRAUGHTS

⚠ **IT'S DRAUGHTS, BUT WITH VODKA, GIN, RUM AND OTHER DEADLY SPIRITS.**

ESSENTIAL SUPPLIES
A chessboard. Spirits. Shot glasses.

All the fun of **Beer Chess** but without the complicated rules, **Booze Draughts** simply replaces the red and black pieces of the traditional game with shot-glasses filled with spirits. To distinguish between the two players, one should drink a colourless spirit (say vodka, gin , schnapps, etc.) while the other should plump for a coloured drink (whiskey, rum, etc.)

Set your glasses out in the usual **Draughts** way and then play the game as usual. This time, however, when a piece is captured by the opposing player, the player that owns the captured piece must **down the glass**. Play continues until somebody either **(a)** wins, or **(b)** falls over.

 **Hints & Tips**

Try not to let yourself get set up for one of those lethal multiple takes. It could be the end of you.

Bolloxed factor...

TOILET DERBY

⚠ **MUCH LIKE A PUB CRAWL, BUT WITHOUT THE 'CRAWLING'...**

ESSENTIAL SUPPLIES
Pubs. Womens/Gents toilets. Beer.

A ludicrous game best played when you've either **(a)** had far too much to drink and you don't care, or **(b)** had very little to drink and you can still run without throwing up. The rules are as follows: **(Men)** pick five pubs in close proximity to each other and, in race conditions, run into each one, hurtle into the Women's toilets, touch the back wall and leave as fast as your legs will carry you. Repeat this process in the next four pubs, the last man to finish, drinks a hefty forfeit. **(Women)** pick five pubs in close proximity to each other and, in race conditions, run into each one, hurtle into the Men's toilets, touch the back wall and leave as fast as your legs will carry you. Repeat this process in the next four pubs, the last woman to finish, drinks a hefty forfeit.

Variants:

Bog Crush. A game that only works when you have a large group of people and a suitably crammed toilet cubicle. The idea is a simple one. **Cram yourselves** into the cubicle one by one. The last person to fit into the space, or the person(s) who can't squeeze themselves in must drink the **alco-forfeit.** (Note: a much cleaner variant of this is the **phone box** game).

Hints & Tips
You're much better off playing this in an area where nobody knows you or your friends. You won't be tracked down then.

Bolloxed factor...
🍺🍺🍺🍺🍺🍺🍺🍺

SNAKES & LADDERS

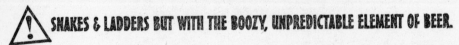

⚠ SNAKES & LADDERS BUT WITH THE BOOZY, UNPREDICTABLE ELEMENT OF BEER.

ESSENTIAL SUPPLIES
A Snakes & Ladders board. A six-sided dice. Some coins. Beer.

Gather a group of friends (up to **six** can play) and determine which one of you will go first by rolling a single die. Whoever gets the highest roll starts first (if two players tie, these players roll again, highest roll wins). The aim of the game is to get to the top before anybody else. Participating players place their tokens (here, read coins – make sure you have a 1p, 2p, 5p, 10p, 50p and a £1) on the starting square and roll the dice to see how many squares they move.

Here's where the beer comes in: **(1)** If a player's token lands at the bottom of a **ladder**, the lucky player can move it to the top of the ladder and the other players must drink a sip (or two sips) per level that the ladder climbs up. **(2)** Likewise, if the player's token lands on the head of a **snake**, the unfortunate player must move his token down to the bottom, consuming one or more sips of beer per level descended. **(3)** If a player's token lands atop another's at the end of their go, both players involved must take a drink from their beers (again, one sip or two). **(4)** On every **Snakes & Ladders** board there is one immensely-long, game-winning ladder, and one terrifyingly lengthy, game-hindering snake. If a player should be fortunate enough to land on the immensely-long snake, all of the other players in the game must

Hints & Tips

You must resist the temptation, once pissed, to try and play the game with real snakes and real ladders. No matter how much fun it sounds.

'shotgun' a beer in his honour. If, however, a player should land on the terrifyingly lengthy snake, this unfortunate soul must **shotgun** a beer himself, from a can pierced once each by the other players. **Note:** the immensely-long ladder and the terrifyingly-lengthy snake don't have to be a cue for shotgunning, inventive players may want to assign a different rule to these two bogey squares, i.e. **Tequila slammers**, enforced nudity, flaming Drambuie, and so on.

The game ends when one player rolls the exact number needed to reach square 100, the winner's square. Anybody who tries to enter the square and fails by rolling **over** the amount needed must drink a gulp of beer **per point**. I.e. if a player sits on square 97 and rolls a six trying to end the game, they overshoot by three (97 + 6 = 103) and so must neck down three gulps of beer as a penalty. When a player finally reaches the winning square, the rest of the players must drink a swig of beer for every level that they are **'below'** the winner. I.e. a player on square 64 is three levels below the top rung and so must quaff three swigs of beer. Lastly, any dice that leave the table during a role, saddle the offending player with a mandatory two-gulp fine.

Bolloxed factor...

267

TOP SHELF CHALLENGE

⚠️ GO INTO YOUR LOCAL BOOZER, GAZE AT THE TOP-SHELF SPIRITS... FEEL THE DANGER.

ESSENTIAL SUPPLIES
A pub. A well-stocked bar. Spirits. Lots of cash.

Simply wander into any pub (as long as the pub chosen has a large spirits supply) and stand determinedly at the bar. Then, from right to left (or vice versa), order a shot of **every spirit** on the top shelf behind the bar. This should deliver an awesome mix of rums, whiskeys, vodkas and gins, each one of which must be downed in quick succession. The winner is the one who makes it to the end of their row of top-shelf death first. (Also known as **The Optics Challenge**.)

Variants:

The Bartop Challenge. Just as the **Top Shelf Challenge** requires you to drink the spirits contained in the Optics bolted to the wall, so the **Bartop Challenge** raises the stakes, daring you to drink the lesser known alcohols that most people have with lemonade, coke or soda. This means drinks like Blue Curacao, Archers Peach Schnapps, Advocaat and so on, plus the less than palatable collection of cordials (which should be imbibed neat) such as blackcurrant, lime, etc. Again work your way from right to left (or vice versa), the winner is the one who finishes his/her assembled drinkage first. If you're feeling kind, you can allow mixers to be used at this stage.

Hints & Tips

This is a game best played in the company of somebody who's just won a fortune at the bookies, and is prepares to pay for everything.

The Beer Pump Challenge. Also known as the **Lager Challenge** for obvious reasons, the **Beer Pump Challenge** works in exactly the same way as the **Top Shelf Challenge** and the **Bartop Challenge**. Starting at the end of the bar that's home to the coke and lemonade gun, simply book your ticket to alco-oblivion by having a pint of each beer or lager that is available on draught. As usual, the winner is the one who can finish the line of pumps first. Players may NOT want to line up the beers, but slowly work their way along the bartop pumps as an evening progresses. Then again, you might not.

Bolloxed factor...

BEERMAT CATCHER

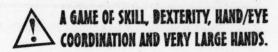

A GAME OF SKILL, DEXTERITY, HAND/EYE COORDINATION AND VERY LARGE HANDS.

ESSENTIAL SUPPLIES
A pub. Some beer mats. A table. Beer.

Simple, yet effective; **annoy** the other patrons in the bar by stealing their beermats and piling the cardboard squares together in the middle of the table. Then, one by one, the players shuffle up to the table, and place a beermat on the lip so that half rests on the table and half hangs over the edge.

Then, in one flowing motion, the idea is to **flip** the beermat up with your outstretched fingers (palm down) and to catch it with the **same hand.** Failure incurs a **one-gulp penalty**. When all of the participating players have done this, the stakes are raised to **two** mats. One mat is placed atop the other and the player attempts to flip and catch the **tiny pile** as before.

When all players have done this, the level of mats **increases** to three, then four, five, six and so on until a **weighty mass** of beermats dares each player to flip and catch it. To **clarify** those rules again:

(1) players must flip and catch the pile of mats with the same hand; **(2)** the player must catch all of the mats in the pile. Even if one slips out, the player's go is deemed a failure and the player must drink.

Hints & Tips

Unlikely as it may seem, water can once again be your friend. Wet beermats tend to stick together better than dry ones, you see...

Variants:

Bar Towel Thwapping. OK, so it's not strictly a variant of **Beermat Catcher**, but taking a beer-soaked bar towel and hitting your fellow man with it, is still a hell of a lot of fun.

Bolloxed factor...

CHEERS!

APPENDIX A

IT'S A FORMAL NAME FOR A VARIED COLLECTION OF BOOZE-RELATED WITTICISMS, ASIDES, QUOTES AND DRINKING JOKES. OR JINKING DOKES. DEPENDING ON HOW MUCH YOU'VE HAD...

BAR JOKES

Lots of 'em...

- It's New Year's eve and a snail goes into a pub and asks for a pint of lager. The barman says: "we don't serve snails" and throws him out of door. A year later to the day, the snail returns to the same pub and says to the barman: "What did you do that for?"

- A horse walks into a bar. The barman says: "why the long face?"

- An aging Irishman moved from his village to another village closer to be closer to the hospital. He went into the local pub and ordered three pints of Guinness. When he

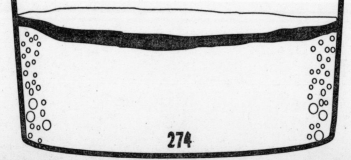

BAR JOKES

drank, he drank one sip from the first pint, one sip from the second, and one sip from the third. Then repeated the process until the pints were empty. He went to the bar for a refill. The barman said, "Ya know me friend, if ya were to drink this beer one glass at a time it would be a bit fresher and bit more enjoyable." The man replied, "Ay, I reckon so, but me two brothers and I agreed to drink our beer this way ever since they left to go live in the States. It's our way of remembrin' one another." The barman replied, "now that makes sense." The man became a regular, but one day he came in and ordered only two pints. He drank those in his normal fashion, sipping from each glass. The other locals and the barman fell silent and hushed. When the man came up for a refill the barman said, "I am sorry about the death of yer brother." The man replied, "Naw, it's noth'n like that, it's just that I stopped drink'n."

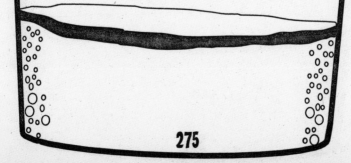

BAR  JOKES

- An Englishman, a Scotsman, and an Irishman walked into a pub together. They each bought a pint of Guinness. Just as they were about to drink, a fly landed in each of their pints and became stuck in the thick head. The Englishman pushed his beer away from him in disgust. The Scotsman fished the offending fly out of his beer and continued drinking it as if nothing had happened. The Irishman picked the fly out of his drink, held it out over the beer and yelled "Spit it out!! Spit it out you bastard!!!!"

- A man walks into a bar and asks the barman for a shot of 40-year-old whiskey. Not wanting to deplete his supply of this rare and expensive drink, the barman pours the man a shot of 10-year-old whiskey and hopes the man won't notice the difference.
The man subsequently downs the whiskey and

BAR JOKES

says "Hey, that was only ten-year-old whiskey. I specifically asked for the 40-year-old stuff." Amazed, the barman reaches into a locked cupboard beneath the bar and pulls out a bottle of 20-year-old whiskey and pours the man a shot. The man drinks it down and says, "Hey, that was 20-year-old whiskey. I asked for the 40-year-old stuff." The barman then goes into the back room and brings out a bottle of 30-year-old whiskey and pours the man another drink. A small crowd has gathered around the man and is watching as he knocks back the latest drink. Once again the man says: "hey, that was 30-year-old whiskey. I asked for the 40-year-old stuff." The barman gives up, disappears into the cellar and brings back a bottle of the good stuff... 40-year-old whiskey.

As the barman returns with the drink, and old drunk who had been watching the

BAR  JOKES

proceedings, leaves the bar and returns with a full shot glass of his own. The man downs the latest shot of whiskey and says, "Now this is 40-year-old Scotch!" The crowd applauds. "Oi, I bet you think you're real smart," slurs the drunk, holding up his own shot glass. "Take a swig of this." Rising to the challenge, the man takes the glass and downs the drink in one swallow. Immediately, he chokes and spits out the pale liquid on the floor. "Ughh!" He exclaims. "That's piss!" "Good guess," says the drunk. "Now tell me how old I am."

• An Irishman has been out at a pub all night drinking. The barman finally announces that the bar is closed, the man stands up to leave and then falls flat on his face. He decides to crawl outside to get some sobering fresh air. Once outside he stands up and falls flat on his face

BAR JOKES

again. So he crawls home, and at the door stands up and falls flat on his face. He crawls through the door and up the stairs. When he reaches his bed he tries one more time to stand up. This time he falls right into bed and falls fast asleep. He awakens the next morning to his wife standing over him shouting at him. "So, you've been out drinking again!!" "How did you know?" The man asks. "The pub called, you left your wheelchair there again."

• The Titanic, on her maiden voyage, has just set sail from England. Every night at the bar, a magician comes on stage to perform amazing and baffling tricks of illusion and conjury. The only problem with the magician's act is that a parrot, which sits on the bar, ruins each trick by shouting out the secret of how the trick is done – "Squark! It's up his sleeve!" or "Squark! He's

BAR JOKES

hidden it in the hat!" Every time, the parrot would do this, and the magician would get madder and madder as the night wore on. Hoping to beat the know-it-all parrot, the magician spent days devising even better tricks in an effort to fool it. One night, the magician is about to perform his newest and arguably his greatest trick, when the ship hits an iceberg and sinks... Fortunately, the magician manages survive, clinging to a door he found floating amongst the wreckage. A day passes and then he spots the parrot, sitting calmly and quietly on a fragment of the shattered bar. The two stare at each other for hours – the magician angry and embittered, the parrot calm and quizzical. Until one day, the parrot can't contain himself any longer and squarks, "Alright! I give up! What have you done with the ship?!"

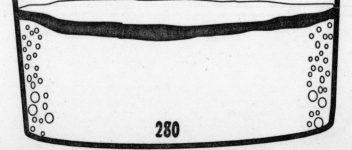

BAR  JOKES

• "A skeleton walks into a bar one night and hops on a stool. The barman asks "What'll it be?" The skeleton replies "get me a pint of Guinness." So the barman gets him his beer and says "anything else?" The skeleton says "Yeah, could I have a mop..."

• Tony and Harold, two fisherman and well-known drunkards, were out in a boat on their favourite lake. Suddenly, Tony got what he thought was a bite. Reeling it in, he found a bottle with a cork in it. Curious, he uncorked the bottle and a genie appeared. The genie said in time-honoured Arabian cliche: "I will grant you one wish." Tony thought for a second and said "I wish this whole lake was beer." Kazamm! His wish came true. The lake was now filled with their favourite brew. Harold looked at Tony in disgust and said "you idiot!! Now we have to piss in the boat."

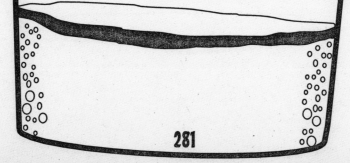

BAR 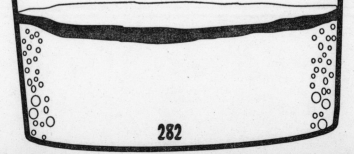 JOKES

• Two drunks are sitting at the bar. One is crying. The other asks him what's wrong. "I've puked all over myself again and my wife is going to kill me." The other drunk says: "do what I do mate. Explain to your wife that some other drunk puked on you. Put ten quid in your shirt pocket and tell her that the drunk was so sorry for messing over your clothes, he gave you some cash to get your clothes cleaned." "Hey, that sounds like a great idea" says the pukey drunk. When he gets home, his wife is angry and begins yelling at him about his clothes. The drunk starts spinning the lie he was told in the pub and says: "look for yourself, there's ten pounds in my shirt pocket." His wife looks in the pocket and finds 20 pounds. "Wait a minute, I thought you said the guy gave you ten pounds for puking on you," says his wife. "He did," says the drunk. "But he shit in my pants too."

BAR 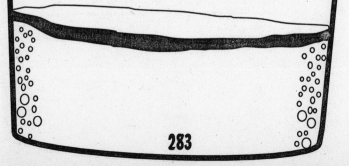 JOKES

• A piece of string walks into a pub, hops on a stool, and says, "Gimme a beer." The barman says: "I'm sorry sir, we don't serve strings here." Disappointed, the string hops down from the stool and goes to the next pub. He hops on a stool and says, again, "Gimme a beer." This barman says: "I'm sorry , we don't serve strings here." The string continues down the row of pubs, stopping in each one to jump up on a stool and ask for a beer. Each time, the barman would reply: "I'm sorry sir, we don't serve strings here." Finally the piece of string gets to the last pub in the town. He's tired, all he wants is a beer. He slithers inside, climbs on a barstool, and says: "Gimme a beer." The bartender says: "I'm sorry, sir, we don't serve strings here." Annoyed, the string sidles outside to think. He's a hard-working string. He deserves a beer. Finally, he comes up with an idea. He twists himself up and musses up his hair, then

BAR JOKES

heads back into the pub. "Gimme a beer!" He shouts confidently. "Hey," says the barman suspiciously, "aren't you that string that was in here a few minutes ago?" To which the string says: "Nope, I'm a frayed knot."

• How many drunks does it take to change a light bulb? Two. One to hold the bulb, and one to drink until the room starts spinning.

• A drunk stumbles out of a pub and is spotted by a policeman. "Can I help you sir?" Asks the copper. "Damn right," slurs the drunk, "somebody stole ma car". The policeman frowns: "where was your car the last time you saw it?" He asks. "It was on the end of this key," says the drunk, holding up his car key. It's at this moment that the policeman notices that the drunk has his dick out. "Are you exposing yourself sir?" Asks the confused

BAR JOKES

constable. "Oh God," yells the drunk. "They stole my girlfriend too!!"

• A Mexican, a Pole, an African American, an Italian, a Priest, a Rabbi, a Nun and a disabled lesbian walk into a bar. The barman looks up and says, "What is this? Some kind of joke?"

• Why does beer go through your body's system so fast? Because it doesn't have to stop to change colour.

• A guy walks into a bar with a large bullfrog on his head. "Where the hell did you get that?" Asks the barman. "Well," the bullfrog replies. "You won't believe it but it started as this little wart on my arse!"

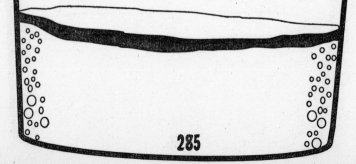

PUB PHILOSOPHY

"Well Bob, you should think yourself fortunate that you still have your liver INSIDE you. My liver and I parted company about a year ago. I can get up in the morning after a heavy night, go down stairs and see my liver sitting there in the kitchen with a big fried breakfast, a fag and a haggard look. Usually, we end up sitting on the couch staring at mindnumbing morning TV. Because neither of us can be bothered to get up and find the remote control..."

• Rehab? Oh yeah right, that's a great game. I'm stuck on Level 7. Isn't that the one with the Undead Flesh-Ripping Tequila-Slamming Mother Superiors of Oblivion. I can beat them, but I'll be damned if I can get past the flying wheelbarrows with the rocket launchers."

• Concerned of Chipping Sodbury says: "What

PUB PHILOSOPHY

most people tend not to realise is that beer is a "gateway drug". By this I mean that anybody who drinks beer on a regular basis, stands a greater risk of becoming involved with more dangerous drugs and narcotics – Heroin, Crack, Mescaline, Valium, the list is almost endless. So stop the madness. Protect yourself by drinking so much that you won't have time for any other drugs."

• Is drinking beer better than sex? Of course it isn't. How can you compare the two? That's like saying that lime cordial is better than sniffing. Of course there's no reason why you can't combine beer and sex for the ultimate experience. Sadly the same doesn't go for sniffing and lime cordial."

• Will continued consumption of alcoholic milk eventually give kids the milk-shakes?"

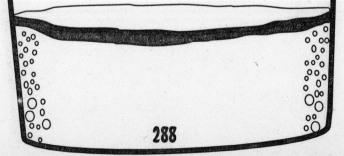

THE FOUR RULES
OF DRIKING

Rule (1) Too much is never enough.

Rule (2) Life is too short to drink low-alcohol lager.

Rule (3) All women are crazy.

Rule (4) Keep Rule 3 in mind and everything they do will make sense.

Did you know: If you hold an empty pint glass to your ear, you can hear the sound of the brewery?

If ever there was a piece of hard evidence that alcohol can make you see clearer, it is this handy tip that appeared in an American newspaper. "Another way to wipe your eyeglasses free of streaks is put a drop of vodka on each lens." Unfortunately, there is no mention of how you go about removing the subsequent lick marks off of them.

MORE PUB PHILOSOPHY

We drunkards hold the future in our hands... so try not to spill beer all over it.

Yesterday, scientists in the United States revealed that beer contains small traces of female hormones. To prove their theory, they conducted an experiment where they fed 100 men 12 pints of beer and observed that 100% of them started talking nonsense and couldn't drive.

• If a hand falls on a piano key, but no one around is sober, does it still make a sound?

Steve looked concerned: "won't your wife hit the ceiling if you come home at three o'clock in the morning, pissed out of your face?" Dave merely shrugged. "Of course she will, she's a terrible shot!"

MORE PUB PHILOSOPHY

See life as it really is. View it through the bottom of an empty brown bottle.

• No mate, I've never tried to get my cat drunk. I am totally against giving animals alcohol, and I'm even more against blowing smoke at them. However, what my cat does in his own time is his own business.

• Yeah, my wife's angry with me again. Just because I woke up last night, got out of bed and pissed in the laundry basket. I mean is that fair? The cat does it too!

THE DRIKERS PRAYER

Give us this day our daily booze,

And forgive us our hangovers,

So we can forgive those who point out what we did the night before.

And lead us not into sobriety,

But deliver us a pizza and a case of beer.

For thine is the pub around the corner,

Open from 7pm to 11pm with the option of a lock-in,

Ah women...

GREAT BEER "QUOTES"

Graffiti spotted in a pub toilet: "You don't buy the drink here, you only rent it." Anon.

• Man, being reasonable, must get drunk; The best of life is but intoxication." G. Byron (Don Juan)

• Drinking when we are not thirsty and making love all year round, madam; that is all there is to distinguish us from other animals." Beaumarchais, P (The Barber Of Seville)

• Work is the curse of the drinking classes." Oscar Wilde.

• I may be drunk, but you are ugly, and in the morning I shall be sober, but you will still be ugly." Sir Winston Churchill

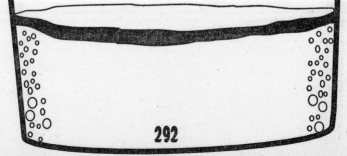

GREAT BEER
"QUOTES"

• Sir, if you were my husband, I would poison your drink." Lady Astor to Winston Churchill. "Madam, if you were my wife, I would drink it." Sir Winston Churchill's reply.

• Reality is an illusion that occurs due to the lack of alcohol." Anon.

• When I read about the evils of drinking, I gave up reading." Henny Youngman

• 24 hours in a day, 24 beers in a case. Coincidence?" Anon.

• I'd rather have a bottle in front of me, than a frontal lobotomy." Tom Waits

• I never drink anything stronger than gin

GREAT BEER "QUOTES"

before breakfast. A woman drove me to drink and I didn't even have the decency to thank her. What contemptible scoundrel has stolen the cork to my lunch?" W.C. Fields

• The problem with the world is that everyone is a few drinks behind." Humphrey Bogart

• You can't be a real country unless you have a beer and an airline; it helps if you have some kind of a football team, or some nuclear weapons, but at the very least you need a beer." Frank Zappa

• Always do sober what you said you'd do drunk. That will teach you to keep your mouth shut." Ernest Hemmingway

• Men are like wine – some turn to vinegar, but the

GREAT BEER "QUOTES"

best improve with age." – Pope John XXIII

• Beer is proof that God loves us and wants us to be happy."
Benjamin Franklin

• I would kill everyone in this room for a drop of sweet
beer." Homer Simpson

• You're not drunk if you can lie on the floor without
holding on." Dean Martin

• The only way to get rid of a temptation is to yield to
it. " – Oscar Wilde

• Men are like wine - some turn to vinegar, but the
best improve with age. – Pope John XXIII

DRINKING LEGENDS

As old as time itself, beer – the foundation of civilisation – has a history that starts in the ancient world and evolves through many types and forms before it reaches the froth-headed pint that you can buy down the local today. Do religion and beer mix? Why did pubs once open at strange hours? Who invented Guinness? The answers to these legendary posers is revealed below...

THE ENGLISH PUB

The idea of the English 'pub' or 'public house' can be traced right back to the rudimentary ale houses and taverns that sprung up during the medieval era – the earliest drinking establishments were literally extensions of the brewers' homes, i.e. they were the 'public' part of the house. The origins of the famous pub signs and pub names are also rooted deep in history. Typically, as the working classes in early England often had no grasp of reading or writing, taverns and inns chose to advertise their presence using pictorial methods. In many cases, landlords plumped for instantly recognisable family crests (leading to pubs like The Red Lion or The Dragon); while others were inspired by traditional folklore (The Green Man is named after a mythical pagan who would cover himself in leaves) or their unquestioning devotion to the monarchy (The King's Head). Additional sources of ancient motivation included reflecting religion in a pub's sign (The Mitre, The Cross Keys); or naming the pub after a local profession or trade (The Baker's Arms). Nowadays, while you still find pubs that nod reverentially to the royals (The Prince Of Wales, The Windsor Castle), most modern pubs are more likely to be named after sports (football, cricket, etc.), famous people or as part of a themed, drinker-friendly chain.

DAVID LLOYD GEORGE

While not a renowned drinker (the Welsh politician was, in fact, an ardent teetotaller), David Lloyd George was the man responsible for some of the UK's more bizarre drinking legislation. The story goes thus: believing that, in 1915, the consumption of alcohol was damaging the war effort, he pushed through the controversial Defence Of The Realm Act which stipulated that pubs were only allowed to open their doors to drinkers at lunchtime and in the evening. Until the late 1980s, these restricted opening hours remained in place, although public pressure has since repealed the law and English pubs, like their Irish counterparts, are permitted to open all day between the hours of 11am and 11pm.

TOBY PHILLPOT

A legendary ale drinker of considerable largesse whose caricatured likeness is immortalised on Toby jugs throughout the land. Think of him as the Oliver Reed of the 19th Century.

ORIGINS

Beer is as old as history itself, its use – as a refreshing, 'safe' alternative to impure water – dates back to Roman Britain, ancient Egypt and beyond. And while early civilisations struggled to preserve fruit and meats, grain grown in the fields was the easiest foodstuff to store. Little surprise then that the versatile foodstuff became the basis for beers and ales, a cheap, easily-produced drink that appealed to both rich and poor alike. According to some historians, the discovery of beer and brewing (and obviously bread) could be responsible for the end of mankind's nomadic lifestyle and his adoption of a static settlement where crops could be grown – thus beer leads to Feudalism, crop rotation, the industrial revolution, computers and so on. And although the first beers were little more than soaked grain, they were widely popular – beer, for example, was often paid to workers in the ancient world instead of cash. Egypt is largely credited as the birthplace of brewing, and its citizens advanced the technique by first 'malting' the grain (leaving it out in the sun to dry, thus releasing the starch and sugar, before mashing it and leaving it to ferment). Food and beer were later combined in 'beer bread', surely the ultimate nutritional combination.

Despite the fact that Egypt's brewing industry was destroyed by a Muslim invasion of the country in the 9th Century, beer-making knowledge had spread far and wide through the Old World – probably by ship to the fringes of what would become Eastern Europe, into Germany, France, Spain, the British Isles and Scandinavia. Only Italy and the more southern countries where grapes were abundant and the weather was warm, stayed with wine- producing – although when they conquered Britain, the invading Romans eventually turned to brewing when supplies of their favourite plonk ran out. And while the early Brits also made alcoholic drinks from apples (cider) and honey (mead), beer quickly became the most popular beverage. In early Europe, beer was brewed at home by women. People would often go to the home of the woman who brewed the best beer to sample it for themselves. Giving rise to the 'public house' or, as we now know it, the 'pub'.

MONKS

While most early beer-brewing was confined to the home, the Christian church was quick to see the potential of the popular drink and jumped into the production of their own booze with extraordinary zeal. From the 11th Century, monasteries throughout Europe became mini-breweries – not only was the beer that was produced sold to travellers, but it became a basic part of the monks' meagre, unspectacular diet. History records that two or more brews were often made from a single malted grain mash; the first would be a full-strength beverage, a beer of high quality reserved for the Abbot, the Archbishop and possibly the nobles that lived nearby; while the second (and possibly third) was much weaker, mass-produced and served up for guests, the poor and the rank-and-file monks. This weak beer was widely used as a milk substitute in the 16th century when disease was rife in the growing towns and cities. So, by the Elizabethan age, beer was being used for both entertainment **and** medicinal purposes.

ELIZABETH I

While today, drinking beer in the morning is unlikely and rare for most of us, in the 16th Century the drink was championed as a health product. Not only did it contain only natural ingredients, but beer was a great source of vitamin B. So while modern man drinks beer for entertainment value, 400 years ago beer was viewed as a relaxant which containing antiseptic characteristics (weak beer barely had an alcohol content above two or three per cent). It is even said that Queen Elizabeth I drank a generous measure of ale every day at breakfast. History notes that she was also very particular about the beer that she drank and would often order in her own supplies of London-brewed ale whenever she went travelling around the country.

LAGER, LAGER, LAGER

You could say that lager was almost discovered by accident. In an attempt to store their beer out of the summer sun, German brewers stashed their beer-barrels in ice-packed caves and basements. They quickly discovered that the yeast behaved quite differently and that fermentation process had been altered by the change of temperature. This 'cold fermentation' process continued to be pursued in central Europe, particularly in the German-speaking states where, in the 16th century, the Purity Pledge was passed, stating that only barley, malt, hops, yeast and water could be used in the production of beer. Naturally, this had nothing to do with the fact that the aristocracy had a monopoly on barley production...

SAMUEL WHITBREAD

Commercial brewing in Britain really took off in the 18th Century, when pubs were drastically outnumbered by growing breweries. One of the early, pioneering brewers was Samuel Whitbread who started brewing Pale Ale at his brewery in Old Street in London in 1742. Whitbread's success was down to a new type of beer, the 'Porter', an unenticing mix of pale ale, traditional brown ale and stale beer (i.e. brew that had matured in its barrel for over a year). Named after the labourers in Manchester and Liverpool, the result was a strong, dark drink that had a caramel malt flavour and a fairly bitter aftertaste. (The Porter style of beermaking continued in popularity until the mid 1830s whereupon competition with mild ale and spirits – especially Gin – caused its favour to wane.)

By 1748, Whitbread had moved to bigger premises to concentrate on the production of his beer. With barely enough capital to get him started, he wisely invested in all of the latest mechanical technology (the steam engine, thermometer, mechanical mashers, etc.), choosing to store his porter-style brews in large vats or cisterns. Keeping the beer this way dramatically reduced the cost of producing it, and Whitbread quickly became rich by supplying his blended beverage to the local pubs and ale houses. If local, pub-based brewing hadn't died out by now, the rise of giant Porter beer tanks that could hold over 3,000 barrels of beer, certainly sounded its death knell. It is said that the famous German brewer, Gabriel Sedlmayer, later visited England in the 1830s to see Britain's brewing technology. He then returned to the continent to add the new techniques to German brewing, thus influencing the development of lager overseas. Of course, brewing on this 'industrial' scale wasn't without its problems. History records that a vat in London's Tottenham Court Road burst in the early 1800's, releasing a tidal wave of beer which demolished the brewery and drowned several people.

ARTHUR GUINNESS

While Samuel Whitbread was making a name for himself in London, an equally ambitious brewer, Arthur Guinness, was poised to embark on a famous career of his own. Come 1759, the businessman sold everything he owned and purchased an old and abandoned brewery in the centre of Dublin. Fortunately, a supply of un-malted barley was included in the brewery deal, but before Guinness could fully malt his stock ready for fermentation, a fire cruelly destroyed the majority of his stores. Without any money remaining to malt the barley, Guinness decided to use what remained of his un-malted barley to make up for the lack of the malted variety. To his surprise, the result was a dry stout, inky black, low in alcohol (about three per cent) and low in calories. The rest, of course, is history. Rich and smooth, the NHS once prescribed two eight-ounce helpings of Guinness to patients as an "appetite stimulant, relaxant, mild laxative and sleep inducer".

PROHIBITION

Hurrah for the 'Roaring Twenties', dubbed as "the greatest, gaudiest spree in history," by F. Scott Fitzgerald, in the US it was a time of rebellious, progressive teens, raging youngsters high on materialism, sex, drugs, and of course, large quantities of alcohol. To combat this outrageousness, the Temperance Movement was established, a campaign to protect the family (and the US way of life) against the damaging effects of booze. Its wide popularity led to the ratification of the Eighteenth Amendment in 1920, a chunk of legislation which prohibited the manufacture and sale of alcohol and effectively established a 'dry' nation. Unfortunately, while in theory Prohibition was designed to defend the innocence of American youth, the law led to hypocrisy within society, government corruption, secret 'moonshine' stills in wooded glades, and an alarmingly high crime rate. The majority of commercial brewers went out of business as a result and only a few survived when Prohibition was repealed in 1933, when the 21st Amendment was passed by a whopping 73% of the government's representatives. Sadly though, the abundance of cheaply grown crops, inexpensive production costs and a desire to keep alcohol content below three per cent, led to the brewing of a collection of bland, watery beers. It's a tradition that still continues today...

THE END